TO: MATTH

Good

year's journey!

The Way Back
to
AMERICA

Howell U U U

June 5, 2014

The Way Back
to
AMERICA

*A 10 step Plan to
Restore the United States to
Constitutional Government*

HOWELL WOLTZ

WOLTZ MEDIA CORPORATION
WILMINGTON, DELAWARE

Published in the United States of America by Woltz Media Corporation
First printing November 2011, Second printing (revised) December 2013
Discounts are available to your company, non-profit or educational
institution for reselling and/or educational purposes.

For more information, please contact the publisher at:
Woltz Media Corporation, PO Box 2216, Advance, NC 27006
Email: info@WoltzMedia.com

This book is dedicated to those who fought so bravely
to create and protect this nation, not only with sword and gun,
but pen. Equal to their courage is that of those who remained at
home and stood by them in their fight, rather than asking those
brave souls to accept the temporary security of tyranny.

ACKNOWLEDGEMENTS

I would like to thank those who helped make this book possible.

Dr. Larry Joel of Louisville, KY, was responsible for getting the original book published in concert with former Federal Magistrate Judge, Arthur P. Strickland, and his legal assistant, Patty Ballard of Strickland, Diviney & Strelka in Roanoke, VA.

Further thanks to my sister, Mary, and her husband, Rob Calvert, in Sag Harbor, NY, who guided and advised on the original manuscript, as well as the lovely lady in my life who wishes to remain unknown. Without these people, this book would not have been possible.

America desperately needs a change of course, and I suggest in these pages that the best and most expedient way of achieving a positive change of direction, is for our government to live by its contract with *We the People*. That contract is known as the United States Constitution.

At present, our federal government is in breach of it.

Howell Woltz

CONTENTS

THE WAY BACK TO AMERICA
A 10-step Plan to
Restore the United States to Constitutional Government

FOREWORD

I love my country without reservation, just not where our leaders (of both parties) are taking it. The people of the United States are like none other in the world, due to our unique mix of cultures and history. The principles upon which our nation was founded are still the best that mankind has ever devised, in my opinion. The problems we face today as a nation, are due mostly, if not completely, to the fact that our leaders no longer follow those principles.

This book was written based on thirty years of research on our Constitution. and how liberty and limited government might be restored. Like an open-source site or code, this book is intended to be the start of a dialogue. Nothing herein is considered proprietary or my idea, as what I propose in these pages is simply that we go back to what worked. These ten steps lead back to what is still the law, according to the United States Constitution. Taking those steps back to law, can reverse the harm done.

We're in trouble as a nation—serious trouble—and it's no one person's fault, but no one person is the solution either. It's going to take *We the People* to fix this mess and we must do it in spite of our leaders and government. Our federal government became illegitimate under its contract with its citizens, as defined in the United States Constitution, long ago. Our elected representatives and courts allowed them to do so. This isn't going to be solved by blaming them, but it's rather clear by now they're not going to provide the solutions either. As Albert Einstein once wrote, "True madness is the belief that the same people, doing the same thing, can achieve a different result."

The people who caused this situation will not be its solution. It's up to us. It's time to turn off the television and start thinking for ourselves now. Terrorism is a great example of our need for independent thinking. The Wall Street Journal reported that between 1989 and 2010, less than 3,900 people worldwide died from terrorist attacks, including the September 11th tragedy in 2001. (NOTE: that number excludes our own terrorist attacks on other nations). To put this specter of terrorism in perspective, eight times more people are killed by lightning each year according to Wikipedia, than all terrorism-related deaths over this 21 year period. That indicates to me that terrorism is little more than another government-created hobgoblin to scare us into accepting the loss of our liberties.

We the People need protection from our own government far more than from terrorists at this point in time. We must stop listening to the siren's song of fear and see what is really happening. We need our Constitution back in force for starters. That was our contract with government.

We've also got to quit fighting with each other over things we'll never agree on. Most of those things have no place as the purview of government under our constitution anyway. They're personal preferences or ideological beliefs which have been cleverly employed by adroit politicians to divide us. We've got to stop letting them do that. We need to be together right now more so than ever in our history. Our future absolutely depends upon it.

While we've been fussing over the small stuff, the politicians, and those who now control them, have stolen our wonderful country from us, as the statistics within will prove. **We the People** are very nearly without a homeland, while Homeland Security, the NSA, and several other non-constitutional federal entities rob us of what little is left us of our legacy as a free people. That's not anger, it is just fact. By dividing us over hot button issues like guns, gays, and abortion, the powerful forces and politicians of both parties, have manipulated us to their advantage and our detriment. Pitting us against one another over things which are guaranteed to pick a fight, while making up shadowy unseen hobgoblins or self-created threats like terrorism to take our rights and wealth, has been a highly potent and successful strategy. It's time to quit reacting and start thinking. Most important right now are our freedom, our solvency, and Constitutional rights as a free people. Let's deal with them first.

By following the steps herein, we can take the nation back to its constitutional path. A copy of the original United States Constitution is included as Appendix A for reference, as many of our nation's founding principles may sound foreign after so many years of government propaganda. Not a single copy of the Constitution was available in my children's schools when I began researching these problems years ago, so it is no surprise that our nation is ignorant of how badly government has breached it. The U.S. Constitution is nothing more than a contract between government and the governed. Our federal government stands in violation of it. It is my opinion this is the reason they no longer want American children to know what it says. When I was a child, a copy was in every classroom. At some point, they all disappeared. That was not an accident.

I propose in the following pages, 10 ways we can fix our nation's problems. Most of these problems can be resolved by simply returning government to the strict limits of our contract. We can argue over the small stuff and social issues once we've saved our country. Ten chapters or Steps lie ahead with distinct, positive actions listed at the end of each one that, if taken, can restore our country to its lawful path, while simultaneously solving every major problem facing it. Sound too simplistic? Please read Step One before deciding. That one change alone could create a different, more wholesome America, by next November.

We must act now and fix our country before we lose our birthright altogether. The following ten steps for restoring the United States to Constitutional government, give a specific blueprint for making that happen quickly, before it is too late.

Howell Woltz, November 8, 2013

STEP 1
RESTORING REPRESENTATION TO THE CITIZENS

The United States of America is a representative-style republic. It is not a democracy as our presidents now like to call it. The word democracy does not appear once in the United States Constitution. We have certain democratic principles, such as the popular election of members of the House of Representatives, but a democracy, we are not. We are a republic.

We elect these representatives from within our respective congressional districts to do our bidding at the national level and to protect our interests so that we may go about our daily lives pursuing our visions of personal happiness, doing so with some reasonable level of domestic tranquility. Our country worked like that for much of our history. The franchise of who was represented was improperly limited, but we have historical evidence that a constitutional America works quite well.

Today, in post-constitutional America, we find ourselves at the opposite end of the suffrage spectrum. Men and women of all colors, creeds, levels of income and education have suffrage (the right to vote), but it is no longer those living, breathing citizens who are represented in Washington.

Rather than serving the people who actually live, work, and die in their congressional districts, most representatives now serve another class of citizen, the corporation. Legislation is overwhelmingly written on their order, and our representatives' activities, votes, and areas of interest, are based on those of corporate and pressure groups that fund them, instead of living, breathing constituents. That is the crux of our problems.

While it is still possible for a citizen to get assistance from his or her representative on mundane matters such as expediting the issuance of a passport, or perhaps getting some help in cutting through the bureaucratic red-tape at the local social security office, it can simply no longer be called a truly representative relationship.

Citizens have no real input or impact on matters of importance at the national level. Their interests, thoughts or opinions are of little consequence or concern to their representative, unless that particular citizen has the ability to write a substantial check to the congressman's re-election campaign. Even then, such influence is quite limited.

In 1874, the Supreme Court ruled in *Home Insurance Co. v. Morse*, that a "Corporation has the same rights to protection of laws as natural citizens." That one decision changed the course of our republic. It began an avalanche of court decisions in favor of monopolists, oligarchs and corporate interests, which continues today. This other class of citizen, the corporation, has, in essence, robbed us of our representation.

In a string of questionably garnered Supreme Court decisions, starting with *Santa Clara County v. Pacific Railroad Co.* in 1886, through *Southern Railroad v. Greene* in 1910, the rights of "citizenship" for these paper fabrications which had no heart, soul or body, became cemented into American law. The court stated in all of these cases, "Corporation is person within meaning of Fourteenth Amendment, which forbids state to deny to any person within its jurisdiction equal protection of laws."

These court decisions, taken directly from the United States Code, are attached as Appendix B. It is difficult to conceive of such a notion as corporate citizenship, until put in context, then it becomes clear it was an outright fraud upon the nation, for which we are still paying the price.

As can be seen in Appendix B, the high court did not make this obtuse decision once or twice, but 14 times between 1886 and 1910 to insure that it could not easily be undone or overturned.

Giving a corporation citizenship is a bizarre and seemingly whacky concept until examined more closely. It then becomes clear it was an evil but brilliant Machiavellian ploy which opened the doors for the monopolists and oligarchs to take control of the nation. For all intents and purposes, I suggest that has now been accomplished.

When corporations became citizens, they gained the right to donate to politicians. That was the reason for their vigorous pursuit of this status. Once established as law, the corporations were able to bribe politicians without an officer of the company going to jail for it, as had been the law from our beginnings as a nation. It was a crime for corporations, unions or special interest groups to buy political support, prior to this decision.

No one has the constitutional right to influence a congressman except a human being living in and/or registered to vote in that congressional district. The Supreme Court made corporate bribery legal back in the nineteenth century, and we see the results today.

For those naive enough to believe that the days of the robber barons and such corruption at the Supreme Court level are over think again.

On January 21, 2010, the Supreme Court kicked out all stops on corporations, unions and PACs (Political Action Committees) being able to buy up politicians in its decision in *Citizens United v. Federal Election Commission*. Foreign corporations and governments can rent or buy our elected officials at all levels of government as well, so long as they stay within prescribed limits. This is not a Republican or Democrat issue, though the judges split along those lines, it is a freedom and sovereignty issue. Whose country is this?

Does it belong to **We the People**, or **Them the Corporations?** At this juncture, the answer appears to be "them".

A few feeble restrictions against such unconscionable bribery were established in 1990 and 2003 at the federal level, but those were gutted by the *Citizens United* decision, along with a 63 year-old congressional ban against corporate and union spending either for or against federal candidates. Restraints have now been eliminated, leaving the nation open for the death knell of our republic as it officially moves toward a corporatocracy.

The very notion that paper boxes in a lawyer's office with some documents and a corporate seal have equal or greater political rights than a flesh and blood human being, while suffering none of the responsibilities of citizenship, is offensive. It is also morally wrong and unconstitutional.

There is not a single codicil or passage in the United States Constitution that mentions corporations, or upon which such constitutional effrontery can be based. Corporate interests certainly cannot claim that such a notion was in the Founding Fathers' vision for the nation either.

Thomas Jefferson, the author of the Declaration of Independence and our third president, wrote: "*I hope we shall ...crush in its birth the aristocracy of monied corporations which dare already to challenge our government to trial by strength, and bid defiance to the laws of our country.*" Jefferson saw and recognized the potential dangers that have come to pass, even then in our nation's infancy.

The deluge of corporate money being thrown at our representatives must stop completely. Only living, breathing citizens, who have the legal right and ability to vote for a candidate, should have the right to donate funds to his or her campaign. There should be no more soft money, hard money, political action committee bribes, or union dues diverted to buy special legislative favors. This must stop. **We the People** must take back our country, and we can never accomplish that if any entity above the individual can buy the loyalty of our representatives, including political parties. A representative's loyalty is constitutionally reserved for the men and women whom that representative was elected to serve.

This is where we must start. This is Step One, and it must be taken soon or the rest won't matter.

The Supreme Court has equated money with free speech, and I have no problem with that. But let me hear that box full of papers with a corporate seal utter just one word or even a syllable. Let me hear it speak. Let me hear it quote the Gettysburg Address or sing the Star Spangled Banner just once. I want to hear it shout for joy at the birth of its child, or weep at the loss of its son or daughter killed in war defending this nation.

Let me see that box of papers with its corporate seal show some sympathy for its fellow citizens rather than only seek a profit for itself. Let me see it render service to its country rather than only to its shareholders and owners. That box of papers is not one of us. It is not *We the People*, whose name is on our contract with government, which is known as The Constitution of the United States. Corporations are not mentioned.

Every war this nation has fought in my lifetime was in service to those cardboard boxes and their corporate seals, not for *We the People*. The corporate citizens don't have their own sons and daughters to send off to war to die for their raw materials, oil, or to seize foreign markets, so they have their pawns in government send ours.

This is possible because they can buy our representatives' hearts and souls with money. Would any honest Congressman vote to send our children to die for some corporate advantage or for barrels of oil we could buy cheaper on the open market? The question answers itself.

Imagine for a moment what our nation's capital would be like if returned to constitutional government. Think of the People's City without the mob of lobbyists, lawyers, and money-changers clogging its arteries and our Capitol's hallways. Imagine 435 men and women quietly and diligently doing the business of their constituents, concerned only with their welfare, rather than being assaulted from dawn to dusk by groups from all over the world with bags of ready cash to buy this legislation or that favor.

What a difference it would make in how they looked at their duties. Just think how very differently our representatives would vote on various issues if they could no longer take money from PACs, parties or corporate-interest groups, but only from the individual citizens back home who elected them.

Think also of the caliber of individual who might run for Congress, if it wasn't just an opportunity to get rich. Holding office would be in service to fellow man, rather than the brothel atmosphere of today where votes are sold to the highest bidders on issues having nothing to do with the lives and needs of those they were chosen to serve at home. If our nation returns to constitutional representation, each issue or piece of legislation would be weighed as to its worth to the folks back home rather than the amount of cash being given by a corporate donor. A far higher level of character and person would be attracted to the job of being a representative.

Monitoring for fraud could not be simpler. Voter registration rolls can be compared with the donor list of each candidate. If any names do not match, or a donor is not a permanent resident within the district, then fraud has occurred. The only exception to this would be military personnel from that district living abroad on active duty, or individual U.S. citizens from that district, living in other nations, who were registered to vote there.

Until constitutional representation is restored where only living, breathing individuals have the right to contribute to candidates, we will not be able to take our country back. Without this step, we are destined to be little more than serfs in a modern-day feudal society, run by the corporations, parties, and PACs, that control our nation's leaders.

While even more preferable that no contributions be allowed at all to stilt the representatives' views, this might preclude some good candidates without personal means of running for office from doing so. There is absolutely no constitutional context, however, for allowing groups, corporations, political parties, or even individuals who are not resident in the district, to give money to someone else's representative. This is what has given corporations, PACs, unions and even foreign groups control over our representatives, and it must stop.

The Constitution of the United States is not just some arcane document, it is a legal contract. It states the terms between government and the governed, and we were the grantors of its powers. The preamble to that contract is quite clear as to who are the parties to it:

> "***We the People*** of the United States, in Order to form a more perfect Union, establish Justice, insure domestic Tranquility, provide for the common defence [sic], promote the general Welfare, and secure the Blessings of Liberty to ourselves and our Posterity, do ordain and establish this Constitution for the ***United States of America***."

Corporations are not mentioned in the entire contract. That is not from some oversight, as can readily be discerned from Mr. Jefferson's quote above. He wished them dead at birth. They simply had no business being involved in government's contract with its masters, ***We the People***, which is why they were excluded from it.

Adam Smith, whom many corporate CEOs would claim as the patron saint of capitalism, despised corporations, calling them "a nuisance in every respect." In his famous tome, *"An Inquiry into the Nature and Causes of The Wealth of Nations,"* he further claimed that corporations caused distortions of free economic activity and tied the "invisible hand" which properly allocated goods and services in a society. Apparently the misdeeds of corporations in England were the source of Thomas Jefferson's fear, and Adam Smith's disdain, of corporations' involvement with government. Of those merchant and manufacturing companies in England, Smith wrote they "have extorted from the legislature... the greater part of our commercial regulations." (Chapter VIII, Book Four, Conclusion of the Mercantile System)

We have seen the same graft and corruption lead our own legislature and high court to turn over our nation to these imaginary citizen corporations, and it has nearly destroyed us. Extortion, bribery and insatiable greed on the part of the corporate oligarchs, has been matched with the desire for power, position, authority and money on the part of those elected and appointed to serve *We the People*.

We must now break this link between greed and power, in order to save our nation. Our representatives must serve only us, the living, breathing citizens, who are party of the first part, *We the People*, in our contract with the United States of America. That contract is The Constitution of the United States. Nothing other than a person can be recognized as *We the People*.

ACTION PLAN

Article I, Section 4 of the Constitution grants the state legislatures the power to prescribe the manner of election of both Senators and Representatives in their respective states. This is the ground where change can be made most effectively and expeditiously at this point in time.

STEP 1- Press for a bill in your state making it unlawful for any persons not resident in a Congressional district, or any group, corporation, PAC, union or political party to give to or spend money on a candidate.

STEP 2- Seek pledges from candidates that they will not accept any funds except from their individual constituents who are residents of their district.

STEP 3- Begin grassroots campaign against the corporations, media companies, and professional organizations that buy your representative's loyalty. Boycott their products, services and members, and let them know why you are doing so.

RESTORING THE GUARDIANS OF LIMITED GOVERNMENT

One key provision of original constitutional design prevented federal government from ballooning into the tyrannical, bureaucratic mess it became after 1913. That provision was the mandated method of electing U.S. Senators.

Article I, Section 3 of the U.S. Constitution states: "The Senate of the United States shall be composed of two Senators from each State, *chosen by the Legislature* thereof, for six years; and each Senator shall have one vote." [Emphasis added] In other words, Senators represented the sovereign States rather than the individuals living in them.

As long as this mandatory method of choosing Senators was followed, there was only so much mischief and damage federal government could do. There was a serious body of leaders, chosen by the elected leaders of the States themselves, to protect the sovereign interests of the States and people, from an expansion of federal powers beyond constitutional limits.

Any senator who did not sufficiently defend the rights of his sovereign State against attempts by the federal government to usurp its powers, would quickly find himself removed and replaced by someone who would. That was an intentional part of the constitutional design and intended protections against centralized federal power.

Thomas Jefferson foresaw what might happen without such a provision, and firmly advised James Madison on the dangers the nation would face.

He wrote: "I do verily believe that if the principle were to prevail of a common law being in force in the United States (which principle.... reduces us to a single consolidated government), it would become the most corrupt government on earth."

Jefferson also wrote, "Our country is too large to have all its affairs directed by a single government." When one considers there were only 13 sparsely populated colonies with 90% of the entire nation's population living within 25 miles of the Atlantic coast when those words were written, their relevance today becomes even greater. Removing representation of the States allowed federal power to consolidate without challenge.

The population of the United States is now over 300 million strong, with 50 states stretching from Maine on the North Atlantic, to Hawaii in the middle of the blue Pacific. The need for more localized, less centralized, governance, as Jefferson recommended, has never been greater.

Instead, the powers granted federal government and many more not granted to it, have been absorbed or assumed in violation of our contract.

Absent tinkering with the Constitution's brilliant design and its delicate balance of power, this could not have occurred. I also do not believe this would have come to pass absent the prompting and funding of corporate oligarchs of the late 19th and early 20th centuries.

The framers of the Constitution were so strongly wedded to the election of Senators by the State legislatures they put that protective mechanism out of bounds to change in Article I Section 4. Congress was allowed to alter the State's regulations regarding elections in many ways, *except the Places of chusing [sic] Senators.* That was not subject to change, and was specifically and clearly intended to always remain the province of, and to be carried out in, the legislatures of the respective States.

The confluence of money from the new corporate citizens, and their agenda of seeking national monopolies, persuaded Congress to violate government's contract with *We The People* in the form of the Seventeenth Amendment to the Constitution.

The proposal was promoted as a populist, *democratic* idea, and became law on May 31, 1913. It also acted to remove our protection against the expansion of federal power, just as feared by the nation's Founding Fathers. Three unconstitutional acts, all passed by Congress within months of each other in the year 1913, can be rightly called the beginning of the end of our republic.

Congress pushed through an unconstitutional federal income tax (The Sixteenth Amendment) and created the privately owned Federal Reserve to print unconstitutional money without the required backing of silver or gold (Glass-Owen Act), that same year, as will be discussed separately in later chapters.

Combined with the Seventeenth Amendment, the Three Horsemen of the Republic's Apocalypse were mounted, and the takeover of the nation by wealthy corporate interests was cemented.

As President Woodrow Wilson later said of these terrible deeds which he helped put in place at the orders of his backers, "I fear I have sown the seeds of my own nation's destruction." Wilson was correct. He had done just that. The United States of the Constitution was debauched and hobbled in service to those who put him in office.

The Seventeenth Amendment changed our Guardians of Limited Government to nothing more than congressmen at large, with little loyalty to rights of State or constituents. It read:

"The Senate of the United States shall be composed of
two Senators from each State; elected by the people thereof, for
six years; and each Senator shall have one vote." Amnd. XVII

While the idea of popular elections for Senators of the States was appealing on an emotional, populist level, the very purpose of the U.S. Senate was negated by so doing. These congressmen at large could be bought and sold by the moneyed interests as their counterparts in the House of Representatives had been since the Supreme Court decisions cited in Step One improperly gave corporations the right of citizenship.

Before the Seventeenth Amendment, Senators were the guardians of constitutional balance and provided the much-needed restraint on federal government exceeding its limits of power. The House of Representatives represented the People, while Senators represented the Sovereign States.

This key component of restraint on government was destroyed in 1913. Power and money flooded to Washington, DC and it has never slowed or stopped since.

A visitor to the nation's capital can visually mark the time-period of the beginning of the republic's demise with a short ride or walk to Georgetown, where everything appears to have sprung in the same era and epoch. That is because most of it did.

At the turn of the 20th century, it was still customary for members of Congress to live in boarding houses while serving their *term* (usually one). With the assistance of a secretary, they tended to the business of their constituents, often slogging through muddy streets to do so. Few wives joined their men in the nation's capital. It was an unpleasant place to be.

As Congressman Albert Gallatin of Pennsylvania once wrote of Washington, DC, "The Federal City is hated by every member of Congress without exception of person or parties." Both power and funds were limited, as intended by the founding fathers, and there was none to waste on unneeded amenities. That was no accident. It was also by *design*.

With the brakes removed from the federal locomotive by the passage of the Seventeenth Amendment, combined with the other unconstitutional acts of 1913 that allowed federal government to tax the people and print valueless paper money, the streets were soon paved with gold, though it was fool's gold to be sure. The party was on and it has never stopped since.

By the time the first hangover from that party visited itself upon the nation in the form of The Great Depression, fashionable townhouses, bars, restaurants and brothels had covered the empty knolls around Foggy Bottoms almost overnight. Hotels were built and filled with wealthy interests buying favors from the nation's elected representatives.

Being a Congressman or Senator changed from public service to a lucrative career for those who could buy or have their way bought into the game and the sovereign States were no longer represented in Congress.

Staffs ballooned from one to 21 over the ensuing decades and wives, girlfriends (and boyfriends) rarely wanted to stay at home any longer. Washington was the place to be.

With every dollar taken from *We the People*, power usurped by federal government, or constitutionally unauthorized law passed by Congress, *We the People* correspondingly suffered an equal reduction in potential income, right of self-governance, and level of personal freedom.

The Founding Fathers knew exactly what they were doing by placing the Guardians of Limited Government as a protective mechanism against such federal power, and the oligarchs knew precisely what they were doing by paying to have that protection removed from the Constitution and taxing the income of the People so that federal power could expand.

Government's Internal Revenue Service has become little more than an armed revenue collector to rob *We the People* of their income, and Congress has done little but take our rights, while distributing much of the booty and power to corporate interests, war profiteers as well as professional unions and monopolies.

For those who consider that assessment to be unduly harsh, I ask only that you review the federal budget for any year since and including 1986 and see where our money goes. Another meaningful exercise would be to study the recent annual reports from our own Freedom House Index, which was established to rank totalitarian nations. By 2010, America fell from number One in freedom when the index began in 1941, to Forty-Third, falling behind many third-world nations and despotic regimes.

Roughly one-third of the 2011 budget ($3.8 Trillion) was squandered on two wars abroad against people who have done us no wrong or harm; prisons for people who do not fall under federal constitutional purview but are incarcerated by it anyway; 16 unconstitutional spy agencies; the so-called War on Drugs (better called the War on Civil Liberties); and the equally unconstitutional Department of Homeland Security, which has done more to reduce the security of our homeland from government tyranny than any other in our history. No one knows the budget of the NSA, but none of the items on the above list (including the NSA) are constitutional, wanted, or needed. Without them, the nation would have no deficit (which was estimated to be over $1.7 Trillion of FY-2011's staggering $3.8 Trillion budget).

The equally bizarre budget for 2012 includes *savings* from a $53 billion high speed rail system (which has yet to be built, and is not a duty of federal government to build) and $336 billion of unseen revenues from job creation for unbuilt highways and a "national infrastructure bank," whatever that may be. (USA Today, February 15, 2011, page 1B, Budget)

The charts from the White House Office of Management and Budget below are self-explanatory. The nation has a serious and rapidly worsening problem.

The path from budget surpluses

Even with proposed trims, the deficit under President Obama's 2012 spending plan would hit $1.1 trillion

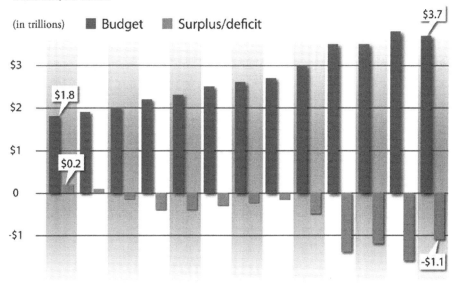

(in trillions)   ■ Budget   ■ Surplus/deficit

$3.7

$1.8

$0.2

-$1.1

2000 2001 2002 2003 2004 2005 2006 2007 2008 2009 2010 2011 2012

Source: White House's Office of Management and Budget

But this whole discussion by federal government of the problem is disingenuous, because it avoids the elephant in the room, which is the national debt. The number is not just $14.1 trillion, though that in itself is a lethal amount. That figure only includes the *public* debt, which is owed to bond and Treasury bill holders, largely foreign, who are now the nation's bankers. What is not mentioned is the incredible $54 trillion borrowed from the so-called Social Security Trust Fund. I say "so called" because there simply is not one. Every penny of income ever paid into this legalized Ponzi scheme has been spent on current expenses since the program began on August 14, 1935. There is no reserve.

This places the national debt at a staggering $68.1 trillion which is a number so large that there is no other expectation except a *crash and burn* scenario. No country has ever been close to such a debt.

The net *public* debt approximated 35% of GDP (gross domestic product or goods and services sold) between 2000 and 2007, but that figure has now doubled and will stay over 70% for at least a decade under the planned budgets and projections.

But the "elephant" which no one mentions, the private debt of government to the Social Security Fund, has already put the federal government's obligations beyond the economic danger zone of 90% of GDP, assuming it pays out accrued benefits.

A recent study by senior fellow and economist Carmen Reinhart of the Peterson Institute for International Economics, of such national crises over an eight-century period, warns that any nation whose debt level exceeds 90% of GDP, inevitably suffers weak growth and high unemployment until that anomaly is corrected. That only makes sense, but no one in our government seems to believe the hard laws of economics apply to the United States.

The U.S. is not the only nation that ever believed itself immune from the hard lessons of history and laws of economics; it is only the most recent one. It not only can happen here, it will.

Perhaps the most reliable economic model of growth factors (and the effects of debt) is that of economist Nikolai Kondratieff. His Long Wave Theory suggests debt will increase until the economy collapses, which he refers to as economic "winter." Debt must be washed out and its causes alleviated before the economic "spring" can begin, just as last occurred during and after our own Great Depression.

The next chart from the White House Office of Management and Budget clearly demonstrates the problem, which is unconstitutional spending. Government's current path will put the nation in a perpetual economic Kondratieff *winter* from which it cannot escape.

Where the money comes from...

$3.7 trillion

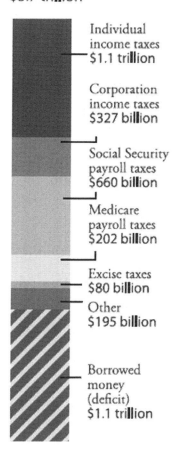

Individual income taxes
$1.1 trillion

Corporation income taxes
$327 billion

Social Security payroll taxes
$660 billion

Medicare payroll taxes
$202 billion

Excise taxes
$80 billion

Other
$195 billion

Borrowed money (deficit)
$1.1 trillion

Where it goes

$3.7 trillion

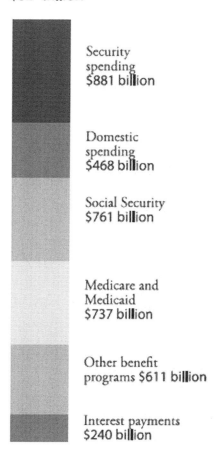

Security spending
$881 billion

Domestic spending
$468 billion

Social Security
$761 billion

Medicare and Medicaid
$737 billion

Other benefit programs $611 billion

Interest payments
$240 billion

Source: White House's Office of Management and Budget

While this may seem a departure from the topic of the chapter (Restoring the Guardians of Limited Government) it is actually evidence as to why we must do so. Without the restraint of Senators who represent the States' interests to keep a leash on federal government, it expanded and usurped the powers and duties of the States and People. That is why this component of the original design of our government, *cannot be changed*, according to the Constitution.

With the Guardians of Limited Government still in place and elected by the State Legislatures as demanded and forbidden to be changed by the United States Constitution, it is my firm belief that the long list of constitutional anomalies that have now brought us to economic ruin, could not have occurred. Senators, representing the States, would have forbidden it.

It is nearly impossible to have the Seventeenth Amendment repealed at this point due to the powers that would align against it, but there may be an easier route via the federal courts, if the nation's mood continues to seek real change. Most Americans have no idea that Senators were ever chosen by their State legislatures, or that the Constitution still requires that method (since it was forbidden from change). The fact that the Framers of the document specifically outlawed any tinkering with that provision, would give great weight to a legal challenge of the legitimacy of that amendment by any of the sovereign States.

Until the American public is once again knowledgeable about its Constitution, or so angry that it seeks real change, this Step back toward legitimate federal government is unlikely to get much traction.

Anger toward government is so great and palpable, however, that this could be that moment. 87% wanted a wholesale change of Congress in 2010, and 78% believed the federal government to be corrupt. After the recent budget crisis (2013), those numbers can only have worsened. There is no doubt a foul mood upon the land.

Hatred and anger are not the solutions. They are just a manifestation that a problem exists. Real change will not come by simply changing one politician for another. A positive, understandable and foundational change must be presented to *We the People*. Requiring federal government to go back to the words of its contract with *We the People* is a simple and strong argument anyone can understand, once they know what the rules were supposed to be and why.

That is one of the purposes of this book. Things have not always been as they are today. The America of my youth and the freedoms we had would seem unbelievable to my children. I hope to see it that way again before they have children. *We the People* must take our share of the blame for letting this happen. We could have stopped it sooner, but many of us did not know the changes allowed by or foisted on our grandparents were illegal. The sins of President Woodrow Wilson are only now being completely visited upon us a century later. But once we have connected the dots and see what has transpired, not acting to undo those evils becomes our own failure, and we can blame no one but ourselves.

The need for reintroducing American citizens to their own form of government has never been greater. Education is still the constitutional purview and province of the Sovereign States, though the federal agenda of the Department of Education has supplanted most if not all local content. Constitutional instruction is one of those important areas where States must reassert their authority to educate their citizens and teach them of their rights and protections from federal authority and abuse. Each young American should be taught about the nation's true form of government to prevent further erosion of our rights. That form of government is a republic, where federal power is limited to a short and very specific list of duties.

ACTION PLAN

STEP 1- The first step is education. Run for, or support local candidates for school boards and state offices, who will work to return local content such as your own State history, as well as training in citizens' rights/constitutional government in the public schools.

STEP 2- Petition local school boards to place copies of the United States Constitution in public school classrooms as they once were and make knowledge of that document and the rights with which *We the People* are imbued (including protections against tyrannical federal government) a part of every school's curriculum.

STEP 3- Once education of the Founder's purpose and the public's need for the constitutional method of electing Senators becomes sufficiently widespread, we must seek 1) the introduction of a proposal in both the legislatures of the States as well as the U.S. Congress, to repeal Amendment XVII, and 2) to concurrently mount a legal challenge of Congressional power to propose and pass an amendment altering this key component of our government's design, when such alteration was specifically prohibited by the Constitution itself.

STEP 4- Develop grassroots campaign and Repeal Amendment XVII movement to increase public awareness of the issue and spark public debate.

A RETURN TO LEGAL SOURCES OF REVENUE FOR GOVERNMENT

Government, at the federal level, has only been able to become so large, burdensome, powerful and over-reaching because of its unlimited source of revenue, even though that source was forbidden to it by the U.S. Constitution. That off-limits source of revenue is us, **We the People**.

In our contract with government, Section 9 of Article I, forbids any "Capitation or other direct Tax" to be laid upon the people. "Government Taxes" were to be derived from the respective States "in Proportion to the Census or Enumeration hereinbefore directed to be taken" as well as "Duties, Imposts and Excises." (Article I, Sections 9, 2 & 8, respectively)

The States with greater populations contributed more, while the less populous paid a smaller portion of the cost of federal government. This mechanism kept federal government lean, efficient, and out of our lives, by design.

When Senators were still elected by the State legislatures as the Constitution requires, they would not allow legislation to pass at the federal level which would put an undue tax burden on the State government that elected them. That would be political suicide.

Members of the legislature back home would view their Senator as having created a political problem for them if they had to raise taxes at the local level where they were elected, just to support a spendthrift federal government wasting money in Washington, DC. A senator who allowed this would have a very short political career.

It was a beautiful self-regulating design the centerpiece, as the reader now understands, being the election of the senators by the state legislators. They had very strong incentives to keep federal spending, power and growth, under tight control. If they did not, they lost their job representing the State in Washington, DC.

The monopolists, oligarchs and owners of corporations with national aspirations, however, sought to have control across state boundaries and at a national level. They could not accomplish that goal with a limited, fiscally-prudent federal government, in a country where each State made its own rules and requirements as to how corporations could operate.

While I have found no hard evidence this element of corporate restriction was part of any planned design, it did have a healthy, restrictive effect on powerful corporate interests. Any expansion into a new State required dealing with its unique laws and rules on a state-by-state basis.

The end of State sovereignty hurt us. There could not be such corporate hegemony if it still existed. We now have the exact same collection of box-brand purveyors of imported trinkets and junk food at every intersection in America, instead of thriving local industries and merchants. The corporate oligarchs of the 20th century knew that State authority controlling them must be removed. They pressed for centralized federal power, so their own could more broadly expand.

Before the curse of centralized federal power, States and local communities controlled their own destinies. If communities did not want local industries, merchants, restaurants and craftsmen ruined by chains and store-brands from other States and nations, that was under their own control. There were no national chains or corporate interests before the cataclysmic changes in 1913 and the rise of federal power. After the Supreme Court overrode the Founders' intent and the Constitution in *Southern Pacific Railroad v. Santa Clara County*, out-of-state corporations could not be denied equal treatment under the high court's bizarre interpretation of the Fourteenth Amendment. Local cultures and economies have been lost to this national hegemony and big corporate interests.

If an individual man or woman had the constitutional right to set up a small hardware store in another state, then a corporation from any state, could set up a large one, regardless of the detrimental effect it may have on the local economy. The view at nearly every intersection in the United States is now the same as a result.

The more powerful the national government could be made, the faster oligarchs, monopolists, and national interests could extend their financial empires and corporate stamp on the nation, crushing local enterprises and purveyors as they spread across the land.

This is a far cry from the humble capitalism envisioned by Adam Smith and his "invisible hand," and it could not have been accomplished without the onslaught of big federal government and control. What we have today is not capitalism, but a dysfunctional *corporatocracy*. The nation is ruled by politicians acting on the whim of large corporations.

The only way to insure their unlimited expansion was to create a powerful national government and environment where a *corporatocracy* could gestate and flourish. That required finding ways of reducing State power and supplying federal government with unlimited funding.

This lengthy introduction brings us to the Second Horseman of Apocalypse, the Sixteenth Amendment to the Constitution, whose passage, once again, directly violated a specific prohibition in the original Constitution against it, by imposing a direct tax on **We the People**, in breach of that contract.

Since that day in 1913, federal government has possessed the power, at the point of a gun, to pick the pockets of the American people whenever it chooses to do so, for any amount. If that sounds like an overstatement, try not paying your taxes and see what happens.

When first researching this questionable creation of a new source of government revenue, two issues troubled me. Primarily, I wondered why monopolists, oligarchs and mega-wealthy men on the order of J.P. Morgan, John D. Rockefeller and Paul Warburg (the powerful men who prompted and largely paid for these efforts) would want an income tax, which they themselves might have to pay. That made no sense upon initial reflection.

The results of the income tax on that group, however, speak for themselves. As of 2008, nearly a century after that federal income tax was put in place; there were 355 billionaires in the United States. That accountd for 45% of the world's total, though we have only 5% of its people. This tax apparently had little effect on that top tier. A case could well be made that the destruction of these critical parts of our constitutional balance actually created the environment that allowed the present discrepancy of income and disparity between today's super-wealthy and the rest of society.

These American billionaires represent over $1 trillion in combined wealth, which is a staggering sum—a thousand billion—between just 355 men and women.

This GAO (General Accounting Office) study in 2008 revealed that nearly two-thirds of the corporations owned and controlled by this group of billionaires, paid zero income tax, even though their combined revenues for that year were in excess of $2.5 trillion.

Corporations as a whole contribute just 7% of federal taxes today, where, as recently as 1943, they contributed 40%. Approximately 90% of stocks, bonds, trust funds, and corporate equity are now owned by the wealthiest 10% of American society, according to the research of Professor G. William Domhoff of The University of California (Santa Cruz). More shocking, this same group who contributes so little now owns in excess of 75% of all non-home real estate as well. Oligarchs and corporations not only control our government, but our country it seems, while contributing only a pittance towards its expenses.

This research led to the inescapable conclusion that those powerful enough to coerce or bribe Congress and The Supreme Court into disavowing their sworn duty to uphold the Constitution, would have little trouble buying legislative protection for themselves against the consequences of those changes. That would be inexpensive child's play by comparison.

The anecdotal evidence and GAO statistics certainly support that theory. Those who benefit from and control 90% of the nation's wealth today contribute almost nothing towards its upkeep. This would have been impossible to accomplish without corporate citizenship, which allowed legalized bribery of legislators to enact changes favorable to them.

We the People got stuck with the tab in the form of the Sixteenth Amendment and its unconstitutional tax on our daily bread, while they eat cake. *We the People* versus *Them the Corporations*. So far, they won.

The second area that troubled me greatly was why *We the People* would have voluntarily supported such an illegal change in our contract. Why would we give federal government the power to dip its hand in our pockets any time it wished to do so? How could such a thing happen?

And that's where the story gets really interesting, because according to Supreme Court case, *United States v. Thomas*, it didn't. "Sixteenth Amendment is effective legal document, even though only four states ratified its language exactly as Congress approved it." (See Appendix C, pages 145-146). [Emphasis added]

So how did it become law of the land if the States altered the wording to avoid passage or refused to vote in its favor altogether?

The law requires each State to exactly replicate the wording of an amendment in it's approval without change, or it is invalid.

The *Thomas* opinion justified this illegal act (and the court's refusal to address it) by stating that "in 1913 the Secretary of State declared it adopted, and Supreme Court follows 'enrolled bill rule' providing that if legislative document is authenticated by the appropriate officials, that document is treated as adopted."

The actual breakdown of what happened can be found in Appendix C in *United States v. Foster*, where the numbers of discrepancies proven by the defendant were listed: "of 36 states tendering Sixteenth Amendment ratifying resolution to State Department, 11 states had adopted versions with different wording, 22 states had altered its punctuation, and one state had actually rejected it." (See Appendix C, page 146)

The 'enrolled bill rule' holds that if the Secretary of State lied about its passage, the Court had to take his word over the hard evidence proving otherwise. In spite of the actual documents showing that the Sixteenth Amendment failed to be properly ratified, the Supreme Court has decided that it is still law. From admitting that only four states properly ratified the Sixteenth Amendment in *Thomas*, the court made a subsequent ruling that effectively put a stop to any further questions, acting to end all challenges by claiming, "Advancing argument, totally unfounded, that Sixteenth Amendment was not ratified by requisite number of states, will result in imposition of sanctions against taxpayer." (*Cook v. Spillman*). In another ruling, "Validity of ratification of Sixteenth Amendment is now beyond review." (*United States v. Benson*).

This led me to the obvious question, "Who was this Secretary of State, with the power to lie to the nation about the passage of a constitutional amendment, without penalty?" The answer: Philander C. Knox.

The next question was, who controlled him? No man could have the unbridled audacity to commit such an act of infamy unless he was absolutely certain he was backed and protected by the most powerful men in the nation if not on earth itself.

And he was. **Them the Corporations** had stacked the deck against **We the People** and Philander C. Knox was their dealer.

More specifically, Philander Knox was the Pittsburgh attorney who put together the world's largest monopoly of that day, U.S. Steel, for J.P. Morgan and Andrew Carnegie. He was the cabal's lawyer and architect of the massive merger of Carnegie Steel Corporation, centered in Pittsburgh; Federal Steel Company, centered in Chicago, the nation's largest; as well as National Steel, National Tube, American Steel and Wire, American Steel Hoop, American Sheet Steel, and American Tinplate. Soon after the merger, American Bridge and Lake Superior Consolidated Iron Mines were absorbed, and more the following year.

Knox was immediately moved to Washington, DC by the cabal to protect its interest as Attorney General of the United States under President McKinley and stayed on under the cabal's next President, Theodore Roosevelt, to enforce the laws, including the Sherman Anti-Trust Act, to fight—monopolies. Not surprisingly, the largest monopoly in the world–his–U.S. Steel, was never touched, and the cabal went so far in 1920 as to garner a Supreme Court ruling that the company was not a monopoly, though there was none larger or more controlling in America.

Knox then went into the Senate to help lay the groundwork for the corporate interests he served. J.P. Morgan and Paul Warburg had greater plans. Knox left the Senate to join their candidate, William Howard Taft, as his Secretary of State to promote "dollar diplomacy". This policy encouraged foreign borrowing from U.S. banks, as a prelude to the creation of the Federal Reserve, which would be founded and owned by the same men.

Taft was not compliant enough for the money trust's interest (though he was still their man) so Woodrow Wilson was brought into the race and nurtured by J.P. Morgan's agent, Colonel Edward

Mandell House, who literally lived in the White House while Wilson was President. To assure Wilson's victory, former President Theodore Roosevelt was also brought back as a third party candidate (Bull Moose Party), to siphon off votes from Taft, which successfully put Wilson (and Colonel House) in office. Even President Wilson referred to J.P. Morgan's man as his "co-President".

By February 3, 1913, there was no one to stop them, and the law which never was—the Sixteenth Amendment—was declared law anyway by departing Secretary of State Philander Knox, though only four States had properly ratified it by the Supreme Court's own admission in *Thomas*.

The Supreme Court has made it clear that it has no intention of following the Constitution or overturning this proven fraud. Attempts by individuals to do so have been wasted and, in fact, proven dangerous.

The researchers who compiled certified copies of each States' ratification documents and published them in a two volume set, *The Law That Never Was*, as example, suffered attacks. One of the authors, William J. Benson, spent many years in prison on tax charges.

States whose documents prove they did not legally approve the unconstitutional amendment could challenge the Sixteenth Amendment, however. The federal government has yet to figure out how to imprison a whole state yet, though Homeland Security and the NSA are no doubt working on it. Without the income tax, neither of them could exist.

If federal government's power to rob **We the People** at will is ever challenged, the shrill cry from such agencies that live from this lifeblood of federal power will be fierce. Moans of gloom and doom will pour from every power broker and beneficiary of this corrupt system, but that is nonsense.

Our contract gave more than adequate sources of revenue for a federal government to provide the services it was authorized to perform. Revenue from the States allocated by census, imposts (a tax on products or services), excise taxes (on things such as liquor, tobacco and luxuries), and most importantly, import duties, to protect American jobs and industries, should all be re-imposed to replace the illegal tax on personal income.

There is no constitutional prohibition against taxation on the income of *corporations*, even without the misinterpretation of the Fourteenth Amendment by the Supreme Court. They are not individuals. Large corporations operating across State lines should pay a federal tax.

For those who wish to hide behind the corporate veil and seek its protection, or spread beyond the natural limits of a man's reach, let them pay a heavy toll for so doing. Not only would this limit the ability of large corporate entities to destroy small entrepreneurs and companies, it would level the playing field and increase diversity of ownership in the economy. That is real homeland security, and once we have accomplished Step One (Restoring Representation to the People), Congress can legislatively correct the court's interpretation of what is and is not a citizen.

A federal tax on large interstate corporations could fall under an excise or impost, without violating the letter or spirit of the Constitution.

As for import duties, they were intentionally put in place by our Founding Fathers and credit for that is likely due Alexander Hamilton. Many of Hamilton's suggestions in his 1791 *Report of the Subject of Manufactures*, such as subsidies and import bans, were deemed unconstitutional by James Madison, but not import duties, which have proven to work.

The United States held fast to its protectionist tariffs and import duties for 134 years before relaxing them in 1926. The vaunted Free Trade movement of recent decades is quite new. Free Trade has now destroyed most of our nation's domestic industries, while helping to further exacerbate disparity in incomes creating a class of super-wealthy. Free trade enriched them beyond imagination, as the GAO figures prove, while sinking the nation that supported them, into a quagmire of debt.

It was not until America became the world's dominant economic power that it suddenly took up the mantle of Free Trade, just as Britain did as the world's leading economic force preceding it. History shows that Free Trade benefits the dominant economic power, but then, it only benefits those corporate interests in the dominant economy which can gain advantage from the importation of cheap foreign merchandise, or those making extremely advanced products which few other nations can produce. Under free trade, however, even those high technology jobs will disappear over time, and eventually, the manufacturing base will be gone, just as we now find ourselves today in post-constitutional America.

What good is saving a dollar on an imported hammer at Home Depot, if there are no jobs left here for *We the People* to earn the money to buy it? Free Trade is for *Them the Corporations*, not *We the People*. The numbers don't lie. Free Trade neither works in practice or theory, except to the benefit of the free traders themselves.

Restoring an effective regime of constitutional import duties would not only provide a legitimate source of federal revenue to replace the tax on personal income, it would create the most dramatic boon to American jobs and manufacturing in the nation's history. Charging duties on imports would level the playing field once more and allow merchandise to be produced and purchased here, by people living here.

There is no downside to exchanging the income tax for import duties except to the importers and purveyors of cheap goods. They have caused our staggering trade deficit and put our people out of work. Any increased cost of goods from import duties and higher costs of production would be offset by not paying income tax. The revived manufacturing base would also be a new source of tax revenue and jobs. Public support roles would plummet as manufacturing returned to our shores.

Historic American import duty rates would more than replace the revenue currently brought in by the illegal tax on personal income, and that revenue could easily support a *constitutional* federal government.

U.S. tariffs ranged between 40-50% until the First World War and were the highest in the world as far back as the Civil War. As Cambridge University economist, Ha-Joon Chang, wrote in his 2008 groundbreaking work on the Free Trade myth, *Bad Samaritans*, "Despite being the most protectionist country in the world throughout the 19th century and right up to the 1920's, the U.S. was also the fastest growing economy."

Import duties not only protected American jobs, they allowed domestic industries to grow and prosper. They will again.

No nation has ever free traded its way into prosperity. Not one. No nation has (voluntarily) become a free trader until its own industries have matured or became competitive in the world economy.

Free Trade serves only the large, powerful corporations that benefit from it, just as the terrorism hoax only serves as an excuse for big, tyrannical government. We need to wake up to both in a hurry before we have no economy or country to save.

Restoring federal government to constitutional sources of revenue would have a curative effect in place of the detrimental drag on the economy now caused by the personal income tax. This would also end the suffering brought to bear on individuals required to pay the income tax, shifting it to buyers of imported goods and luxuries instead.

Income tax is not only harmful to the nation, it is unconstitutional. It was foisted on **We the People** by outright fraud. There is nothing we can do about that and The Supreme Court has proven itself useless in correcting it, I believe, in service to big government and those who put them on The Supreme Court as seems evident in the cases in Appendix C. It will once again be left to *We the People* to fix this in spite of our so-called leaders. They have become little more than minions for corporate and professional interests. That is not said out of anger, it is just the way it is.

Federal government's ability to pick the pockets of *We the People* must end or our nation and what's left of our freedom will. That's the choice. Government will only remain limited as long as its sources of revenue are *limited* as well.

The answer lies in taking back our representatives from their corporate masters as discussed in Step One, and forcing them to legislatively undo this constitutional anomaly of a tax on income by calling for a constitutional convention to end it.

Article V of the Constitution authorizes the legislatures of two-thirds of the States to call for a convention to make such a change. Three-fourths of them must then ratify the change. Thirty-eight States can force the federal government to undo this wrong against *We the People*. The Constitution provides adequate means of raising revenue for legitimate services federal government is legally allowed to provide and perform. Those are exceedingly limited as will be discussed ahead.

ACTION PLAN

STEP 1- Reinstate constitutional sources of revenue, beginning with imposts, excise taxes and especially import duties. That will have the immediate effect of rebuilding our domestic industries and returning jobs to America. As the income tax is phased out, any remaining revenue needs can be allocated to the States to raise, if needed, to fund legitimate federal government expenses, as provided in Article I, Section 2 of the Constitution.

STEP 2- Call for a constitutional convention at the level of State legislatures as well as by Congress, to repeal the Sixteenth Amendment. Vote only for those candidates at State and federal level who support that effort.

STEP 3- Begin grassroots campaigns to pressure State governments that did not properly ratify the Sixteenth Amendment to challenge its legality and legitimacy. As sovereign members of the Union, States could not be attacked for bringing suit against federal government, as individuals have been. According to the *Thomas* decision, only four States did properly ratify it, though doing so violated Article I, Section 9 of the Constitution, which prohibited such a tax. Only a legal challenge by the States could be effective at this juncture.

STEP 4- Impose income taxes on large corporations, but only those that reach across State or national boundaries, or are over levels of targeted incomes. This will act to level the playing field and protect small businesses and entrepreneurs who provide 2/3 of American jobs, while keeping them competitive with the larger corporations.

RETURNING TO CONSTITUTIONAL MONEY

In the watershed year of 1913, the Third Horseman of the Apocalypse of our republic appeared in the form of the Glass-Owen Act. It was better known as the Federal Reserve Act, though what it created was not federal and it certainly was not a reserve. In fact, it was quite the opposite. It was a private central bank, owned by the world's wealthiest individuals, who were granted the power to print currency without any backing, outside of law and in violation of the United States Constitution.

It was a license to create money of no real value, to fund the growth of federal government beyond all natural economic and constitutional limits, at a tidy profit to its private owners.

This was not the United States' first experiment with what is kindly called *fiat currency*—money of no real or intrinsic value—it was its fourth.

The other attempts at circumventing constitutional requirements for legal tender all ended in disaster. This last one, The Federal Reserve, may cost us our nation altogether, if it hasn't already. The hole the private bankers have dug for us this time may be too deep to crawl out.

The Federal Reserve has for all intents and purposes, already caused the nation's bankruptcy. Congress discharged *all* debts not payable using *Federal Reserve notes* on June 5, 1933, and it became law (House Joint Resolution 192). The nation could no longer pay its obligations in *constitutional* currency. This took only 20 years to occur under the monetary authority of The Federal Reserve (1913-1933). The United States has, in essence, been under Chapter 11 bankruptcy ever since. Gold ownership was suspended, and all legal debts "heretofore and hereafter incurred" could only be paid in printed currency of no value.

Central banks *are not for the benefit of the nation's people,* as history has proven. They *are for the benefit of those who own or control the central bank,* and the political/financial elite they serve.

The first central bank in America was chartered by the Continental Congress in the spring of 1781, before the Constitution was drafted. It was called *The Bank of North America* and was fraudulent from the start. When its founder, Robert Morris, couldn't raise the initial capital ($400,000), he used his political influence with Alexander Hamilton to make up the difference. Morris was allowed to take gold the United States borrowed from France, and deposit it into his new bank. He then created *fiat* money against the debt (not the gold), which he loaned to himself and his associates for the required cost of subscription in the bank.

By 1783, just two years later, it was shut down by President George Washington. This failure, combined with the nation's pre-revolutionary experience with the un-backed *Continental* dollar, led to the constitutional prohibition against such currency of no real value in Article I, Section 10.

The crisis precipitated by the Continental was still fresh on the nation's mind when the Constitution was written. Due to that failed national currency and the States' own un-backed currencies, inflation reached 5,000% between 1775 and 1779. This eventually happens to all such *fiat currencies,* including the Federal Reserve notes of today.

George Washington wrote in 1779, "A wagon load of money will scarcely purchase a wagon load of provisions." In a letter to his friend and revolutionary general from France, Lafayette, George Washington wrote:

> *"We may one day become a great commercial and flourishing nation. But if in the pursuit of the means we should unfortunately stumble again on unfunded paper money or any other similar species of fraud, we shall assuredly give a fatal stab to our national credit in its infancy."*

In spite of these experiences and failures, Alexander Hamilton was back in 1790 with a proposal for a second experiment with private central banking, incorrectly named, *The First Bank of the United States*. It was operational by 1791, but again employed the same fraudulent capital scheme as its predecessor, by borrowing government money to pay the capitalization. The bank's biggest critic, among many, was Thomas Jefferson. He publicly called Hamilton's hand on the fraud, declaring, "Call it by what name you please, this was not a loan or an investment, but an outright gift."

As is always the case with un-backed or fractionally backed currencies, wholesale prices rose by 72% in the ensuing five years and public outcry began against it. The charter was not renewed in 1811, and the nation's second central bank was closed.

Undaunted, the financial schemers and money-changers were back by 1816 with another plot. Congress chartered *The Second Bank of the United States*, (though it was America's third).

Again, inflation spiked and the economic roller-coaster that always attends such un-backed currency tormented the nation until President Andrew Jackson put an end to it. He ran for re-election in 1832 on the slogan, "Bank and no Jackson, or no bank and Jackson."

The charter was not renewed. The nation then entered an unparalleled era of real prosperity which lasted until the National Bank Act of 1863 created not one, but many, nationally-chartered banks, to print unbacked currency for the War Between the States.

In a private letter to William F. Elkins on November 21, 1864, President Abraham Lincoln wrote of the money power involved:

*"The money power preys upon the nation in time of peace and
conspires against it in time of adversity. It is more despotic than
monarchy, more insolent than autocracy, more selfish than bureau-
cracy. I see in the future a crisis approaching that unnerves me
and causes me to tremble for the safety of my country. Corporations
have been enthroned, an era of corruption will follow, and the
money power of the country will endeavor to prolong its reign
by working upon the prejudices of the people, until wealth is
aggregated in a few hands, and the republic destroyed."*

President Lincoln's dire predictions have come to pass. The
rapacious takeover of the nation by corporations was a *fait accompli*
within decades of Lincoln's murder. Taking control of the nation's
currency via The Federal Reserve was the *coup de gráce* and death
of the American republic for all practical purposes.

Money and power continued to collect in fewer and fewer
hands just as Lincoln predicted, throughout the following century.
By 1979, the top .1% earned 20 times the income of the bottom
90%. By 2006, the disparity between the richest .1% and the bottom 90% had grown to 77 fold.

The nation, today, "is in a few hands, and the republic
destroyed," just as Lincoln feared it would be. The corporations
had "been enthroned" by the Court and our currency came under
their private control.

This could not have happened with constitutional money, which
has real, intrinsic value. It grows organically and steadily, and does
not lend itself to concentrations in the hands of few in a free nation.

The United States Constitution authorized the federal government "To coin Money," and "fix the Standards of Weight and
Measures" in Article I, Section 8. Article I, Section 10 specifically
prohibits the sovereign States from making "any Thing but gold
and silver Coin a Tender in Payment of Debts." There are no
exceptions. All four of America's central banks have been nothing more than ploys by men of extraordinary wealth and their

politicians to circumvent the United States Constitution for personal gain.

The concept of central banking is quite simple. Since government cannot legally make worthless cash under its contract with **We the People**, Congress has authorized its wealthiest donors to do so and they are paid handsomely for doing it. Congress has mandated that the fraudulent cash is legal tender for payment of debts, in direct violation of the passage cited above from the United States Constitution, requiring gold or silver.

The worthless cash is of value only because no other means of exchange is allowed, by law. Direct access to newly printed currency is limited to government, large banks, and large corporations when it initially enters the economy. Every new bill printed reduces the value of every one already in existence, and they all become worthless as time goes by.

As Eighteenth century French writer Francois-Marie Arouet Voltaire wrote, "Paper money always returns to its intrinsic value, which is zero." If $10 are in circulation and one more is added, each one of the existing dollars becomes worth only $.90, and so on. At present, the Federal Reserve is creating $1 trillion additional notes each year, liquidating the value of every outstanding federal reserve note by 10% per annum. Meanwhile, the corporations, banks and wealthy, who have had access to the new additional cash when it enters the economy (via the nation's largest banks), have made profits from this added money up front, before it liquidated the value of the remaining money supply. That leaves the inevitable devaluation to be absorbed by **We the People**.

The devaluation of our money is nothing more than an insidious tax. As John Maynard Keynes, one of the architects and proponents of fraudulent money admitted in his 1919 treatise, *The Economic Consequences of the Peace*:

> *"There is no subtler, no surer means of overthrowing the existing base of society than to debauch the currency. The process engages all the*

hidden forces of economic law on the side of destruction, and does it
in a manner which not one man in a million is able to diagnose."

While sometimes called the "Science of Money" to occlude its real purpose, it is common fraud and it is in violation of the United States Constitution.

The effects of this fraudulent process can be explained as easily as mailing a letter. In my own lifetime of 59 years, a simple government postage stamp has increased from just $.04 to $.46. This represents an 1150% rate of inflation, or more correctly put, The Federal Reserve has made my dollar worth less than $.09 in less than six decades. The cost of delivering my letter has not *increased*; the value of my *money* has been fraudulently *decreased*. I've been robbed by a pair of thieves: The Federal Reserve and the U.S. government. They stole my dollar and left me a dime in its place. Soon, I'll have nothing left. All of my wealth and value will have been transferred by fraud to the .1% who controls government and our country today, and I will have paid for the party.

That's the "Science of Money." That's *fiat* currency. That's the Federal Reserve, and that's fraud, the biggest one ever in mankind's history.

Hopefully, the problem created by The Federal Reserve is now clear. Along with the Sixteenth and Seventeenth Amendments, all passed in 1913 at the prompting of the same powerful men who would own the private central bank, our prospects as a free republic became questionable.

The Guardians of Liberty, our State-elected Senators, were removed by the Seventeenth Amendment to allow federal government and corporate power to expand without limit or restriction. A private central bank was created by the Glass-Owen Act, giving the power to print money of no value to the most powerful men in the corporate and banking world: J.P. Morgan, Paul Warburg of the

Netherlands and Germany banking family, John D. Rockefeller, and the Rothschild dynasty of England and France.

The Sixteenth Amendment, put into law by their attorney, Secretary of State, Philander C. Knox, gave government the power to tax individual Americans, to ensure payment of their enormous fees for making fraudulent money in their private central bank, The Federal Reserve.

As Lord Lionel Walter Rothschild, the son of Nathan Mayer Rothschild, heir to the original Rothschild (Mayer Anselm Bauer), was fond of saying, "Permit me to issue and control the money of a nation and I care not who makes its laws."

Once the Rothschild, Morgan, Warburg and Rockefeller coalition controlled America's money through the Federal Reserve, they also did not care who made the laws, as they could control them. John D. Rockefeller's father-in-law, Senator Nelson Aldrich, ran the Senate Banking Committee, and his New York bank chairman, Benjamin Strong, was put in as the first Chairman of the Federal Reserve. The nation belonged to the corporations, just as President Lincoln had feared and foreseen in his letter to William F. Elkins in 1864.

It is time to take our nation back. The best place to begin that process is by removing control of the nation's money supply from the private central bankers, and returning our country to constitutional money.

The problem once again becomes political and educational. Few Americans have taken the time to understand this process. Politicians are also going to be hard to convince that it is time to end their spending orgy.

The means to solve these perplexing problems were provided by three brilliant men over the past quarter century. They include senior Professor of Economics, Walter E. Williams, (George Mason University); Congressman and presidential candidate, Dr. Ron Paul; and central banking historian and constitutionalist, G.

Edward Griffin (author of *The Creature from Jekyll Island: A Second Look at the Federal Reserve*). These men graciously took the time to discuss these matters with me in interviews over the past 22 years, while I was doing research for this book.

They concur the first step is to repeal all 'legal tender' laws, which require the citizens (under the threat of imprisonment) to use and accept these fraudulent, unconstitutional *Federal Reserve notes*. Professor Williams has thoughtfully added the suggestion that all taxes on gold, silver and platinum transactions must also be eliminated to make their use as medium(s) of exchange feasible again. By taxing *real* money, government makes its use impractical and expensive (by intent). Professor Williams reasons this well, "so there would be no other forms of money, and the government monopoly would be reduced and hence the ability to tax—some would say steal from—us through inflation."

This would free up the public to innovate other means of exchange as well, and put competitive models in place. That would be a good start.

Next, the United States Mint was designed to coin the public's gold and silver at little or no cost, in standard weights and measures (a dollar is defined as 371.25 grains of silver in The Coinage Act of 1792). Government was not intended to *provide* money, but to produce it from private wealth, guaranteeing only that it was of proper weight and purity.

This needs to be its purpose again. The mint should resume free coinage of the public's gold and silver as currency. Gold must be established as an auxiliary money reserve at free-market value, with only silver at a quantity per dollar. If our society must have a currency, it needs to be a real one. We should also be free to create and use other means of exchange.

In spite of our leaders' malicious drowning of our nation in debt, we must honor those obligations. The federal debt should be paid, completely, using additional Federal Reserve notes printed solely for that purpose. Those obligations were made with the lenders' understanding and expectation that they would be paid with *Federal Reserve* notes, so there would be no fraud by doing so. In order to comply with and honor the Constitution while putting an end to lawless money, all *Federal Reserve notes*, including the extra and final issue to pay off all government debt, must be backed by the nation's reserves of gold and silver.

One of my advisors, Ed Griffin, suggests withholding the military's stockpile of gold. I respectfully disagree, if one still exists (See Note at end of chapter). It would allow our presidents to continue getting the nation in more trouble abroad, if real money were available to them. After the last several administrations' unilaterally declared wars, Mr. Griffin might now agree.

When Mr. Griffin made his original calculation of the value of a *Federal Reserve note* in his landmark book, *The Creature From Jekyll Island: A Second Look at The Federal Reserve*, it was based on 1993 figures. One *Federal Reserve note* was equal to .0047 silver dollar, or differently stated, it took 213 *Federal Reserve notes* to make one real or *constitutional* dollar.

Using his same formula, I replaced those numbers with debt and money supply figures from 2006, when writing the first version of this book. The value was already less by two-thirds and rapidly dropping. It took 726 *Federal Reserve notes* to equal one real dollar, just 13 years after Mr. Griffin developed the formula. That was before the budget-busting printing spree and banking/corporate giveaways of the years between 2007-2010, but the increase in gold's price has offset the effect to a great extent.

As of July 14, 2013, the Federal Reserve places the money supply at $10.629 trillion (http://www.federalreserve.gov/releases/h6/current/), and it is adding $1 trillion per year. The U.S. Debt Clock showed the United States Debt as $16,915,664,597,843 at 3:15 PM that same day, and growing so fast I had to pick the last four digits (http://www.usdebtclock.org/).

The U. S. government's gold supply is estimated at 260 million ounces according to Forbes Magazine's recent article by Todd Ganos,(http://www.forbes.com/sites/toddganos/2013/07/07/ is-gold-really-worth-40000-per-ounce/). Gold is not the standard under our law, silver is, but gold is a real store of value. Silver stores have been depleted or coined (see Note at end of chapter) but we will use the 1993 level to be conservative in our estimates. Gold is currently selling for 64 times the price of silver ($19.779/ ounce), so that will be its valuation for this calculation. Inventories of U.S. gold and silver generously become valued at:

Silver- 320,000,000 ounces @ .7734375 oz./real dollar = $ 413,737, 374
Gold - 260,000,000 ounces @ 64 times silver   = $329,122,560,000
Value in real dollars   = $329,536,297,374
Liabilities against that value, however, are 83:1.

Debt (07/14/2013) $16,915,664,597,843
Outstanding currency $10,629,000,000,000
                                 $27,544,664,597,843

($27,544,664,597,843 : $329,536,297,374 = Ratio of 83 dollars in debt, to every real dollar in value held by government)

If the estimated $54 trillion in unfunded payments to the American people for Social Security, Medicare and Medicaid are included, then that ratio becomes 248:1. Would any bank loan $248 dollars against $1 in assets? Not likely, and soon, this will occur to the foreign nations who buy our debt as well.

Once the final printing of *Federal Reserve notes* necessary to fulfill all existing government debts and obligations is completed, a debt-free nation must move forward, spending only its revenue derived from legal, constitutional taxes and sources. By limiting its funds, this should force Congress to live by Article I, Section 8 as well as the Tenth Amendment which precludes them from any activity not listed therein. That could put an end to overreach into areas where federal government has no legal authority.

Once backed by the nation's gold and silver stores, the trillions of *Federal Reserve notes* in circulation around the world will have a real value and can be used as money until they are retired, but the American people can no longer be *forced* to use this unlawful money at the point of a gun as is the case today. Government will have to accept *Federal Reserve notes* as payment for its taxes or any other obligations, and they can be used with other members of the public as long as the other party is *willing* to accept them. Real money, however, would also be available for commerce, ending the harmful boom-bust cycles and constant erosion of value inherent with the *fiat* money of no real value manufactured by The Federal Reserve of today.

The Federal Reserve System itself would then become nothing more than a private check-clearing service for banks, without any monetary authority, and have no further power to lower the value of our money. As John Stuart Mill wrote in 1848 of debt issuers, they "*may have, and in the case of a government paper always have, a direct interest in lowering the value of the currency because it is the medium in which their own debts are computed.*" This debauchery is theft, and it must stop.

ACTION PLAN

STEP 1- Repeal the Federal Reserve Act (Glass-Owen) and all legal tender laws requiring the use or acceptance of federal reserve notes, except that government must accept them for taxes and payments.

STEP 2- Abolish all taxes on gold, silver and platinum transactions, so they may be used as money, without additional transaction costs or fees.

STEP 3- Reopen the United States Mint for free coinage of the public's gold and silver, basing the value of a "dollar" at 371.25 grains of silver (.7734375 troy ounces), as required to be the standard under the United States Constitution and law.

STEP 4- Establish gold as an auxiliary money reserve at free-market value, coined at specific weights, but not denominated in value, to float against the silver "standard" dollar.

STEP 5- Print or electronically create a final run of *Federal Reserve notes* to pay all United States debts and obligations that were incurred in the fiat currency, and pay them off using those *Federal Reserve notes* printed for that purpose.

STEP 6- Use all federal holdings of gold and silver to back the *Federal Reserve notes* issued and outstanding to make them constitutionally legal money for continued use until retired, but allow no more to be created.

STEP 7- Free the American public to create its own means of exchanges, including barter, product and service exchanges, private and/or electronic digital currencies, and any other means they choose as a free people.

Note: According to the Silver Users Association, the United States store of this metal may already have been liquidated: "In the early 1980's, the U.S. government's strategic stockpile of silver was locked in by law at 139.5 Million oz. Congress has since authorized legislation to dispose of these stockpiles. In late 2000 the U.S. Defense National Stockpile Center delivered its remaining stockpile of nearly 15 Million oz. to the U.S. Mint for coinage programs. Since 2001, the U.S. has had to purchase silver for its coinage programs from the open market. This has boosted silver consumption by 1% annually." Source: (http://www.silverusersassociation.org/silver/uspolicies.shtml)

STEP 5

RETURNING GOVERNMENT TO CONSTITUTIONAL DUTIES AND LIMITS

Arguments having been made for what got our nation in trouble (and suggestions made for how to extricate ourselves), it is proper to discuss what federal government is *supposed* to do for **We the People**.

What are its legitimate duties? What, if any, are its limits?

The answer to the first question, "What are its legitimate duties?", can be summed up in two words, "very few."

The federal government is extremely limited in its duties and they are all specifically listed in Article I, Section 8 of the United States Constitution.

"What are its limits?" They are stringent and exact. Anything not listed in Article I, Section 8 is forbidden as a duty of federal government. Unless positively stated as its function in the Constitution, the Tenth Amendment of the Bill or Rights precludes federal government from it. James Madison's words were clear:

"The powers not delegated to the United States by the Constitution, nor prohibited by it to the States, are reserved to the States respectively, or to the people." AMENDMENT X, UNITED STATES CONSTITUTION

By turning to Appendix A, the actual duties can be seen and read as James Madison wrote them. They are few and limited. In essence, they allow federal government to raise money for its own operation, through specified means; organize a navy to provide for the common defense; and to carry out duties which would be expected at the union level, such as postal service, courts for disputes between citizens and governments of different States or nations, establish treaties, and develop a common set of standard weights and measures. (See Article I, Section 8 in Appendix A)

If needed for defense, and only then, an army could be raised for no more than two years by calling up the State militias. That is only if Congress voted to declare war, which has not happened since World War II.

Federal government can regulate interstate commerce to keep it open and free, set up a patent office, and punish crimes external to the United States such as "Piracies and Felonies committed on the high Seas, and Offenses against the Laws of Nations". It can also "provide for the Punishment of counterfeiting the Securities and current Coin of the United States," to protect the integrity of money and government securities.

That is all. The alphabet soup of federal bureaucracies such as the DOJ (Department of Justice), FBI, NSA, EPA, FDA, Homeland Security, sixteen spy agencies, our standing army, and all the rest whose powers are not specifically granted in Article I, Section 8, are *unconstitutional*.

They are not listed and are therefore precluded by the Tenth Amendment from being a duty of federal government.

There is not a one of them we would not be better off without in reality. Not one. Even if one of them were of any positive value, their very existence is unlawful. Those duties belong to the States and people, not federal government.

The best description of the separation and limitations between federal powers and those withheld solely for the States and people can be found in the words of the Constitution's main author, James Madison:

> *"The powers delegated by the proposed Constitution to the federal government are few and defined. Those which are to remain in the State governments are numerous and indefinite. The former will be exercised principally on external objects, [such] as war, peace, negotiations, and foreign commerce....The powers reserved to the several States will extend to objects which, in the ordinary course of affairs, concern the lives, liberties, and properties of the people."*
> *The Federalist #45*

There can be no question as to the Founders' intent when the author of the Constitution stated it so clearly. Federal government was to be lean, efficient and kept out of the nation's internal affairs. It was to be as removed as possible from the daily lives of the citizens. The critical areas of day-to-day governance were held to be the province of the States. Federal government was then precluded from exceeding these strict boundaries by the *Constitution* and is clearly in violation today.

The preponderance of power was, by contract, to remain with the sovereign States and **We the People**. Federal government was to deal with externals such as defense from attack; while the States, were delegated authority over internal matters that affected the people.

Since the advent of the Three Horsemen of the Apocalypse in 1913, however, Congress has inserted itself into every nook and cranny of the private lives of its citizens, though contracted to leave us alone and protect us from such tyranny by others.

From the moment the federally-controlled radio station on the alarm clock comes alive as the morning wake-up call, through the morning cup of federally-taxed coffee and the drive to work on federal highways paid for by federal gasoline taxes; until the end of the day, where over half of the average American's daily wages will be robbed in some other form of tax, the federal government has wormed and intertwined itself into the lives of its citizens' every move, moment and dollar.

The federal government of the United States of America has become that against which it fought for most of our nation's history.

As the comic strip character in *Pogo* once said, "I have seen the enemy and it is us."

The once-revered *land of the free* cannot stay atop its own index created to judge others, as briefly referenced in Chapter 2. The vaunted Freedom House, founded in 1941 by Americans concerned with the advance of fascism, has reluctantly dropped its own founding nation to Forty-third place, well behind many of those it once criticized and vilified for the same practices now employed by the United States. (Annual Report-2007)

The attendant report entitled, "Today's America: How Free?", cites the now-familiar abuses for which the United States is known today, such as its secret torture camps around the world, "extraordinary rendition" (illegal kidnapping), broad and uncontrolled wiretapping by the NSA and other federal entities, and the rise in the number of documents classified and kept from **We the People**, which the study states, "has jumped from 8.7m in 2001 to 14.2m in 2005....a 60% increase over 3 years."

The study excoriates the criminal justice system which has replaced America's once-respected and admired federal judiciary. It has become little more than a conviction machine for the 14,000+ federal statutes with prison as a penalty. The study cites the explosion of the number of citizens in American gulags from "1.39 per 1,000 in 1980 to 7.5 in 2006."

The United States now leads the world and all of human history in the number and percentage of its citizens in prison. With only 5% of the world's population, we now hold 25% of its prisoners. No dictator, tyrant, or *evil empire* has ever come close. Many human actions once considered poor behavior, or no crime at all just a few years ago, are federal offenses in post-constitutional America. The *land of the free* has become The Incarceration Nation, and the prison industry its fastest growing.

This 2006 study came before the true number of American prisoners was exposed by Senator Jim Webb (D-VA) in March of 2009. In a national article in Parade Magazine, Webb disclosed the nation's secret:

"1 in 31 Americans are in the corrections system today. Either we are the most evil people on earth or we are doing something very wrong."

The real number of Americans in its penal colonies and corrections system according to Senator Webb was 7.3 million, with 2.3 million currently behind bars, a record for human history. Communist China incarcerates one of every 1,272 of its citizens. An American citizen is over thirty-six times more likely to be in his nation's corrections system than a communist Chinese citizen, to put that in perspective.

Our federal government has become that from which they were designed to protect us. We have seen the enemy, and it is in Washington, DC.

As can readily be seen in Article 1, Section 8, most of the statutes fabricated by Congress to send Americans to prison, exceed federal constitutional authority. Federal government does not have legal jurisdiction.

Our so-called leaders have turned the nation into the very definition of a police state. There are currently over 18,000 separate police agencies operating within the United States. Though many nations are far more populous than the United States, none has ever had such an astounding number.

Every new law passed by Congress *reduces* human freedom. Every new agent of government *increases* the chances of suffering it. Every new prison is filled to satisfy its corporate and union beneficiaries.

Prison is now America's fastest growing industry, and there is a connection. The numbers would indicate more than just a "connection" and more on the order of a takeover of the nation. The United States now has:

1. The highest percentage of citizens in its penal system (1 in every 31 adults; 1 in 9 have been; and approximately 1 in 4 have a criminal record, according to the Department of Justice, as of 2010)
2. The highest number of police agencies of any nation in human history (18,000+)
3. The highest overall number of people in its penal system of any nation in history, by multiples (7.3 million)
4. The highest number of criminalized behaviors of any society in human history. (14,000+ at the federal level alone. Title 18 has over 4,000 criminal statutes, but Congress has also created in excess of 10,000 civil regulations to which it has assigned the criminal penalty of imprisonment)

These numbers are so outrageously skewed to the extreme that they leave all (other) police states in history a distant second. For those who contend that this cannot happen in America, I would suggest the figures above prove that it already has. We have seen the enemy, and it is our own representatives in Congress who have done this to **We the People**. *They* should be imprisoned for such senseless violations of our Constitution and freedoms. There is no excuse for what they have done.

Please turn again to Appendix A and read the short list of authorized duties of federal government in Article I, Section 8. They are very few. It will not take long. Then read the Tenth Amendment once again here in this section or in Appendix A, which restricts federal government to only those duties as a matter of law. That is about as clear as it gets. Federal government was never authorized to have such powers.

Congress had no power to create but a handful of these laws, and no authority to create the vast majority of federal agencies which police them any more than the Executive Branch had the power to create its Department of Justice, its NSA, its FBI, or its 16 spy agencies, as will be discussed in the next chapter.

Many of the States' legislatures are finally beginning to listen to their citizens on this federal abuse. *We the People* had enough long ago.

In the relatively moderate State of Oklahoma, House Joint Resolution 1089, sponsored by Representative Charles Key, passed by an overwhelming 92 to 3 in 2008. It put the federal servant-cum-master on notice.

The resolution stated:

"Whereas the Tenth Amendment defines the total scope of federal power as being that specifically granted by the Constitution of the United States and no more; and whereas, the scope of power defined by the Tenth Amendment means that the federal government was created by the states specifically to be an agent of the states; and whereas, today in 2008, the states are demonstrably treated as agents of the federal government..... Now, therefore, be it resolved by the House of Representatives and the Senate of the 2nd session of the 51st Oklahoma Legislature: that the State of Oklahoma hereby claims sovereignty under the Tenth Amendment to the Constitution of the United States over all powers not otherwise enumerated and granted to the federal government by the Constitution of the United States. This serves as Notice and Demand to the federal government, as our agent, to cease and desist, effective immediately, mandates that are beyond the scope of these constitutionally delegated powers."

Such action by Representative Key and the Oklahoma House of Representatives is a template for all other sovereign States. The Oklahoma Senate did not have the courage to follow through on the resolution (and went into recess to avoid it) but public anger over federal government's destruction of the nation and our liberties will force them to act at some point, or such cowardly legislators will lose their seats one day.

This resolution serves as an excellent template, however, for our ACTION PLAN, and should be implemented in every state.

ACTION PLAN

STEP 1- Pressure state legislators to introduce and pass resolutions in their respective assemblies, putting federal government on notice of its breach of contract. Order it to cease and desist in its unlawful activities.

STEP 2- Organize grassroots campaign to elect Representatives who will fight to repeal all of the 14,000+ laws which are not under federal government's purview as defined in Article I, Section 8, and are prohibited by the Tenth Amendment from being under federal purview and authority.

STEP 3- Support and elect candidates for the U.S. Senate who pledge to recommend only candidates for federal judgeships who:

> A- Have never been a prosecutor, and;

> B- Will pledge to dismiss any criminal charges or convictions under laws which are not rightfully the purview of federal government, as is their obligation under law and Constitution.

STEP 4- Support only candidates for Congress who will pledge to eliminate agencies of federal government not specifically authorized by the U.S. Constitution to speed an end to federal control of our lives. The Tenth Amendment precludes the national government from such involvement. That is the law.

NOTES ON STEP 5

"The general rule is that an unconstitutional statute, though having the form and name of law, is in reality no law, but is wholly void, and ineffective for any purpose; since unconstitutionality dates from the time of its enactment, and not merely from the date of the decision so branding it. No one is bound to obey an unconstitutional law and no courts are bound to enforce it."

16 Am Jur 2d. §177. late 2d. §256

"An unconstitutional act is not law; it confers no rights; it imposes no duties; affords no protection; it creates no office; it is in legal contemplation, as inoperative as though it had never been passed."

Norton v. Shelby County, 118 US 425, 30 L Ed 178, 6 S.Ct. 1121 (1886)

"Where rights secured by the Constitution are involved, there can be no rule making or legislation which would abrogate them.", Miranda v. Arizona. 384 US 436, 16 L Ed 2d 120, 105 S. Ct. 1602 (1966)

"All laws which are repugnant to the Constitution are null and void." Marbury v. Madison, 5 US 137, 2 L Ed 60 (1803)

RETURNING THE EXECUTIVE TO CONSTITUTIONAL RESTRAINTS

The position of President and Chief Executive of the United States, under the constitutional confines of Article II at any rate, is a rather mundane job, except perhaps in time of war.

A *constitutional* president has little power. He signs legislation written and approved by others, has the power of appointments to certain posts, and is titular head and Commander of the nation's defense forces, but only when an actual war has been officially declared by Congress.

Article II, Section 2, is clear about when this duty is held: "The President shall be Commander in Chief of the Army and Navy of the United States, and the Militia of the several States, when called into actual Service of the United States." Only Congress can do that, and absent a declaration of war, starting a war is a violation of law.

It is Congress's job "To declare War", "To raise and support Armies," "To provide and maintain a Navy", and "To provide for calling forth the Militia". (Article I, Section 8, U.S. Constitution) It is even the job of Congress "To provide for organizing, arming, and disciplining, the Militia, and for governing such Part of them as may be employed in the Service of the United States." (Ibid) So even as Commander in Chief, there is little for a *constitutional* president to do. Congress has the responsibility for most of the real work.

The president can also "make Treaties" but only "with the Advice and consent of the Senate... provided two thirds of the Senators present concur." (Article II, Section 2, U.S. Constitution)

The president can "receive Ambassadors and other Public Ministers", "take Care that the Laws be faithfully executed", and "shall Commission all the Officers of the United States." The only other constitutional duty he has is to "grant Reprieves and Pardons for Offenses against the United States, except in cases of Impeachment." (Article II, Section 2, U.S. Constitution)

A *constitutional* president is clearly one with plenty of time on his hands, who has almost no effect on the lives of the people of the nation, nor was he or she supposed to. The President is a figurehead. Any other powers outside of these listed are forbidden to the President by the Tenth Amendment of the U.S. Constitution. This is the law. This is how it is supposed to be, but this is not how it is today in post-constitutional America.

The Executive Branch has assumed duties and powers never authorized or imagined by the Founders and their constitution, and in many cases, in direct opposition to it.

From the constitutional role as a somewhat insignificant figurehead of a severely limited federal government, the office of President of the United States has been illegitimately expanded to the most powerful position in the world. Its misdeeds and abuses have the potential to affect every life on earth, and to even end life on earth as we know it.

Aside from being completely outside of our nation's own laws and government's legitimate limits, it is dangerous to the world to have one man or woman, a politician at that, with such power over mankind as a whole.

Should the nation begin to edge back from the brink of disaster, the first to be reined in and pulled back from the cliff must be the President of the United States of America: not any one of them in particular, but the office itself. It is far too powerful and it is in contractual breach with the People who granted government and president their powers in the first place.

From this limited base of legal duties, the presidency now manages sixteen unconstitutional spy agencies, has a national police force (FBI), an internal spy agency (National Security Agency), and legislates from the White House using a tool with no basis in law called an executive order.

Presidents now start unilateral wars (e.g. Kennedy-Cuba, Reagan Grenada, Bush I-Panama, Clinton-Bosnia, Serbia, Haiti; Bush II-Iraq and Afghanistan; Obama-Somalia and Pakistan). They break treaties instead of making them, debase the currency instead of protecting it, sanction the murder of "Ambassadors and other Public Ministers" rather than "receiving" them, and oversee the most powerful standing army in the world, none of which is legal or constitutional.

The abuse which feeds the misdeeds of the presidency more than any other is the unconstitutional *executive order.* That is a power not found in Article II and is therefore forbidden. It is a means of by-passing Congress and usurping its powers, but as the presidency has also became the titular head of a political party (another anomaly not anticipated by the Founding Fathers) it becomes less and less likely that Congress will challenge presidential authorities that have expanded beyond constitutional boundaries.

Congress's own activities and legislation can rarely find root in Section 8 of Article I, as is required by the Constitution as well, so they are in poor position to challenge unconstitutional Executive authority. That would be the pot calling the kettle black. The Supreme Court, as will be discussed, has been scared of its own shadow since Chief Justice Hughes caved in to President Franklin D. Roosevelt in 1937, and has shown no stomach for challenging either branch or preserving the Founders' instituted restraints. We are now left without the wonderful system of constitutional checks and balances as designed, and have only willful blindness by each branch of government to the other branches' illegitimate behavior, in my opinion, out of fear of being challenged on their own.

The first of these unconstitutional *executive orders* or proclamations was issued by Abraham Lincoln in 1861 at the outbreak of the War Between the States. It suspended the writ of *habeas corpus*, which is the most basic protection of individual liberty. This is the right to be brought before the court to challenge illegal detention. (Article I, Section 9, U.S. Constitution)

"The presidential act was challenged by Chief Justice Roger Taney who, in the case of *Ex parte Merryman*, vigorously contended that the power of suspension resided only in Congress. Lincoln ignored the order of the court". Presidents have been using the illegitimate tool, legislating from the White House, ever since.[1] Some of the most dangerous seeds of the nation and world's potential destruction have been sown by U.S. presidents using this power which they don't have under law or their contract with **We the People**. There is no such power as an *executive order*.

President Theodore Roosevelt used this illegitimate tool to establish his federal bureau of investigation (FBI). In 1907, he asked Congress to create this national police force, but was rebuffed by the legislature, which correctly informed the president there was no such authorization in the Constitution. That was not (and is not) an allowed duty of the federal government.

Undaunted by constitution, law, or Congress, President Roosevelt created his national police force using the fraud Lincoln once employed to suspend the constitutional privilege of *habeas corpus*—an *executive order*.

In 1908, Roosevelt put his illegal operation under the purview of his attorney general, Charles J. Bonaparte, descendant of French Emperor, Napoleon Bonaparte, and its agents were promptly caught going through the mail of Roosevelt's main opponent,

1 *Encyclopaedia Brittanica, Vol. 5, Micropaedia, p. 601*

Senator Benjamin Ryan "Pitchfork" Tillman,[2] who "became such bitter enemies that at one point the President barred Tillman from the White House."[3]

Roosevelt's FBI was unconstitutional then, is unconstitutional now, has never been authorized by Congress, and it is still snooping through private citizens' mail (and worse) today, a century later.

The next President Roosevelt, Franklin Delano, created the OSS (Office of Strategic Services) in June of 1942, to coordinate the constitutional intelligence gathering functions of the army and navy, under William J.("Wild Bill") Donovan.[4]

The OSS was dismantled at the end of World War II in October of 1945, but government had tasted the forbidden fruit of unsupervised spying.

When Harry S. Truman succeeded Roosevelt as president, he "established by *executive order* a Central Intelligence Group and a National Intelligence Authority. The bodies selected key personnel from the motley group assembled under wartime pressures by the OSS and tried to impose some central direction on postwar intelligence operations, although the armed forces maintained their independent intelligence services."[5]

This "motley group" as the Encyclopaedia Brittanica kindly describes these characters, reports directly to the Executive Branch, which illegally created their organizations outside of constitutional authority using means not found in law. The CIA has been responsible for wars, murder and mayhem, ever since, in the name of whomever was president at that time. The encyclopedia credits the CIA with such international terrorist acts as "the

---

2 *Walker, Samuel. Popular Justice: A History of American Criminal Justice,2nd Ed. (1997) Oxford Univ. Press, p. 139*

3 *Encyclopaedia Brittanica, Vol.11, Micropaedia, p. 776*

4 *Ibid., Vol. 3, p.28, Central Intelligence Agency*

5 *Ibid.*

expulsion of Mohammad Mossaddeq as premier" [of Iran] in 1953, "the toppling of an unfriendly leftist government in Guatemala," in 1954, and "the attempted Bay of Pigs invasion of Cuba," in 1961. The encyclopedia also briefly mentions the revelation that "former CIA operatives had reputedly played illegal roles in the Watergate affair."[6]

The Brittanica Encyclopaedia was chosen as the source for much of this information, as the information itself has the potential to be inflammatory, and is far less kindly handled by other sources.

What the encyclopedia fails to share with its readers is the fact that the legitimate leader of Iran, Mohammed Mossadegh, whom the CIA deposed under Kermit Roosevelt's direction (President Theodore Roosevelt's grandson), was Time Magazine's *Man of the Year* in 1954. He was responsible for taking back control of his nation's oil resources from British Petroleum, which had stolen them by force of arms under the British Army. His crime was taking back resources stolen from his nation by a foreign army, for a private corporation, at the point of a gun. This sounds oddly familiar.

The CIA's Guatemalan escapade referenced by the encyclopedia was its overthrow of democratically elected President Jacobo Arbenz, so dictator Colonel Carlos Castillo Armas, could be installed to do the CIA's bidding. Each of these acts is terrorism by the definition of the term stated by United Nations Secretary General, Kofi Annan, after the 9/11 attack in New York in 2001.

Recent books revealing these misdeeds are chronicled and supported in M.I.T. Professor Noam Chomsky's tome, *Failed States*, and by former company insider John Perkins in *The Secret History of the American Empire*. These two well-known and reliable authors detailed from public records or personal knowledge, that the executive branch and its CIA have participated in many murders, overthrows, terrorist actions and attempted coups. A list of the various terrorist acts of the presidency and its spy force gleaned from these

---

6 *Ibid.*

two books, include the attempted overthrow in 1963 of Abdul Karim Qasim by CIA operative, Saddam Hussein. Saddam failed, so the CIA executed Qasim on TV by firing squad, much like its hanging of Saddam himself 40 years later. It then sponsored the killing of 5,000 innocents.

Other incidents reported and confirmed by Perkins and Chomsky include the 1964 overthrow of Victor Paz Estenssoro, president of Bolivia, Three years later, CIA agent Felix Rodriguez illegally entered the country and murdered Argentine Che Guevara in La Higuera, Bolivia. Salvador Allende was overthrown by the CIA in Chile (1973), just as they had over thrown President Joao Belchior Marques Goulart of Brazil a decade earlier. President Jaime Roldos of Ecuador was assassinated in a CIA-coordinated plane crash in 1981, as was Omar Torrijos of Panama, that same year.

More recently, President Hugo Chavez dodged two CIA/ Executive Branch attempted murders and an overthrow. The bitter backlash from these acts of terrorism have fueled the animus now seen against the United States by these same nations and should be no surprise. It is no wonder Venezuela has offered (NSA) Eric Snowden sanctuary. Murdering and over-throwing duly elected heads of states to take control of their natural resources or to install a puppet dictator not of that people's choosing, are not things quickly or easily forgotten, any more than Americans will easily forget the attack on New York by Saudi Arabians on September 11, 2001. The bitter fruits of America's terrorist activities are coming back to haunt it.

But international crime by the Executive Branch has not been limited to South and Central America alone. In 1963, President Kennedy ordered the assassination of our ally, South Vietnamese President Ngo Dinh Diem. Recently, Ken Saro Wiwa and 8 other environmentalists were hanged under Executive/CIA pressure for standing up to Shell Oil (and the CIA) in Nigeria. Presidentially sponsored terrorist activities have taken the United States from the most respected and trusted nation on earth, to last place, tied with its one-time arch-enemy, Russia, as the least-trusted and most dangerous, according to Noam Chomsky in *Failed States*.[7] France and Communist China have taken the nation's place as most respected and trusted, in recent international polls. Even Mexico, our closest neighbor, sees the United States as the most dangerous nation on the planet, according to polls cited by Chomsky.

The man who coordinated much of this terrorist activity for presidents over recent years, from Chomsky's research, was John Negroponte. Negroponte ran covert operations and terrorist training out of Honduras under the Reagan administration. President George W. Bush made this man Deputy Secretary of State under Condoleeza Rice, who was seriously considered as a draft choice for the Republican candidate to face now president, Barack Obama in 2008. The United States was only a nomination away from having a man considered by many nations as the Western world's equivalent of Osama bin Ladin, as its representative to the other nations of the globe.

Prior to his appointment as Deputy Secretary, Negroponte headed and coordinated the activities of all sixteen of the executive branch's unconstitutional spy agencies, not one of which has ever been authorized by Congress. They were created by *executive order*, because they were illegal.

Perhaps the most insidious and unquestionably, the largest of these shadowy organizations is the NSA (National Security Agency) which was created outside of constitution and law in 1952 by President Harry S. Truman, again, using an *executive order*.[8]

Even the most flattering and mundane description of this agency, whose principle activity is spying on the American people, infers its illegality, as now confirmed by Eric Snowden, the recent

---

7 *Chomsky, p. 28*

8 *Walker, Samuel. Popular Justice: A History of American Criminal Justice,*
2nd ed., Oxford University Press. (1997) p. 138

NSA whistleblower. The Encyclopedia Brittanica entry states: "The NSA grew out of the communications intelligence activities of U.S. military units during World War II. *The NSA was established in 1952 by a presidential directive, and not being a creation of Congress, is relatively immune to Congressional review; it is the most secret of all U.S. intelligence agencies..... the NSA maintains no contact with the public or the press."* [9] [Emphasis added]

There is no place in a free nation for such undercover organizations, be they one or sixteen, with or without reasonable congressional oversight and review. They are illegal, unconstitutional, and far more dangerous to the nation than any protection they purport to offer it.

These surreptitious, lethal and illegal groups are also unnecessary. Provision for appropriate, *constitutional* intelligence gathering, under the proper oversight of Congress, has always been available through the legal department of naval intelligence.

Starting offensive wars, murdering foreign leaders, and training terrorists are not appropriate functions of a constitutional United States government. Such crimes have put the nation at risk by having been sanctioned and carried out by our Presidents over the past 60 years. This *must* stop.

The true purpose of these sixteen secretive spy agencies, and the military, according to author, John Perkins (who once served them) is to act on behalf of what he dubbed America's "Corporatocracy". He wrote, "Our military is not a defender of democracy, but rather an armed guard for exploitive corporations."[10] The NSA, on the other hand, is here at home to spy on us. There is no excuse or constitutional authority for such an agency.

This has all had a corrosive effect on freedom and a chilling one on the press, which is freedom's canary in the coal mine. "The United States was ranked #53 on the World Press Freedom list in

---

9 *National Security Agency, Encyclopaedia Brittanica, Vol. 8, Micropaedia, p. 550*

10 *Perkins, John. The Secret History of the American Empire, p. 291*

2006 (compared to #17 in 2002) and has been severely criticized by Reporters Without Borders and other NGOs for jailing and intimidating journalists."[11] Leaving the executive in charge of the military instead of Congress when it is not at war has also led to disaster and must cease. Only in a war *declared by Congress*, when the military has been called to service, does the control of the nation's forces transfer to the president, *instead of Congress.*

Every president who has started a unilateral war or violated a treaty, to which the United States is a party, should have been impeached and removed from office. That would sadly include every president back to and including, Harry S. Truman. Until Congress finds the courage to challenge the Executive Branch on its infringements and violations, which have so endangered the nation, the United States will remain on a self-destructive course toward tyranny. It is these fabricated, often wholly created conflicts, which give government cause and support to take our liberties, which it purports is being done to protect the nation's citizens. Aside from being illegal, that is a distasteful, dangerous, and very poor bargain.

Twentieth century writer and journalist, H.L. Mencken, wrote of this farce, "The whole aim of practical politics is to keep the populace alarmed (and hence clamorous to be led to safety) by menacing it with an endless series of hobgoblins, all of them imaginary."

Sixty years of immoral and flagitious skullduggery by the CIA and its 15 bastard sister agencies have created some real hobgoblins and bogeymen since Mencken's day, but stopping the overt acts which have caused this hatred of our nation is the surest way to end it, rather than piling on more of what caused it with murder (by drone) and worse.

Cessante causa, cessat effectus. When the cause ceases, the effect ceases.

---

11 *Ibid. Perkins. p. 295*

And while ending the bloody hell of *spy v. spy* and world wars may sound utopic, only the nation's so-called leaders have dragged us into them as revealed by recently discovered history. The nation was duped, tricked or spurred into the last century of wars by leaders doing so to serve corporate interests, bankers, and more recently, the military-industrial complex itself (Lusitania-WWI; Pearl Harbor-WWII; "communist threat"-Korea and Vietnam; "weapons of mass destruction"-Iraq; "terrorists"-Afghanistan, Pakistan, Ethiopia, and Somalia, to name just a few).

Change can come, with a return to constitutional government, and as Victor Hugo once wrote, "Greater than the tread of mighty armies is an idea whose time has come." The fruits of an Executive Branch exercising unconstitutionally granted powers are too bitter to bear much longer. It is time to put the presidency back in its place. The time for this idea *has come.*

The usurpation of control of the military from Congress by the Executive Branch combined with the establishment of unconstitutional spy and police agencies are frightening and potentially deadly aspects of unconstitutional executive powers. *All* powers not listed in Article II, however, must be yielded by that branch, to return it to *constitutional* bounds and limits. Congress must find the courage to impeach those Presidents who violate law and our contract, and remove them from office.

The majority of executive departments and agencies now under Executive control are either constitutional functions of Congress, the Judicial Branch, or unauthorized as duties of federal government altogether. This can no longer be overlooked if we are to return to legitimate federal authority and a separation of powers.

Of the 15 Executive departments, only the Department of the Treasury, Department of State, Department of Commerce (for international trade) and Department of Defense—only in time of declared war—are legitimate areas of executive power. The rest are without authority or are self-granted.

Possibly the biggest mistake our Founders made was not listening to their oldest and wisest member, Benjamin Franklin, when he proposed that the Executive Branch be run by a three-man committee, so power would not collect there as it has. The difference such a small change could have made in our nation is unimaginable... the wars avoided, the temperance of ego-driven and politically-motivated decisions which have taken us from the path of liberty. The steadying hand of other opinions would have changed history.

Perhaps one day *We the People* will have to implement this plan of Benjamin Franklin to save ourselves from the political collection of executive power which has done so much harm to our country. Take any election of the past century and imagine how much better off we would be by having the top three contenders as a committee, rather than just one man running the nation, whose first loyalties were to his political party and staying in power rather than to *We the People*.

It would truly be a different, and in my opinion, a far better, kinder, and safer world.

ACTION PLAN

STEP 1- By force of congressional action, confirm the invalidity of *executive orders*, and make such Executive legislation an impeachable offense.

STEP 2- Authority over any agency of government, independent or quasi-independent department, commission or body, which was created outside of constitutional authority and the legislative process, must be assumed by Congress for liquidation, or conformation to a constitutionally authorized function of federal government found in Article I, Section 8.

STEP 3- Presidential authority over the military is clearly defined as only existing during time of declared war. Congress must reassert its constitutional authority over the military, and remove any Executive Branch control, except when the President assumes the title of Commander in Chief, during an officially and constitutionally declared war.

STEP 7

RESTORING JUDICIAL BRANCH TO CONSTITUTIONAL FUNCTION

For most of the first century of the nation's history as the United States, the Supreme Court was situated in the basement of the Capitol Building in an unused sub-committee room.

In fact, the need for a federal judiciary in a government of such limited powers was itself questionable. The original plan had been to make the High Court a sub-department of Congress to bring out only in the rare instances where issues fell under its purview, such as boundary disputes between the States or to punish a counterfeiter. External affairs, such as piracy, or an American violator of the laws of other nations, were also its purview, but little more.

The Judicial Branch was set apart in the end by the Constitutional Convention under Article III, to act as a part of the checks and balances of government and as a monitor of adherence to the Constitution by the Executive and Legislative branches. The Supreme Court did not hear or review a single case its first year, it only monitored congressional legislation.

The system worked well. Legislation was vetted for its compliance with the Constitution as it was being written, which had the effect of limiting mission creep by federal government up until the 1860s when the Court left its sub-committee room in the basement of Congress and moved into its own lavish quarters.

Things have gone considerably downhill since then.

While the famous case of *Marbury v. Madison* in 1803 is credited with establishing the principle of judicial review that was a de facto and intended result of working with Congress in close quarters under the same roof in the early days. The justices prevented unconstitutional legislation from becoming law in the first place. It worked then, and could again.

Marbury v. Madison confirmed the principle, which already existed that, "All laws which are repugnant to the Constitution are null and void."

Had the Supreme Court continued this practice of reviewing legislation prior to its passage, either informally or formally, the explosion of illegal government incursion into areas of the citizens' lives where it has no legitimate authority, could have been largely avoided.

The Supreme Court's practice, since its physical separation from the lawmakers in the 1860s, has been one of review long after the passage of unconstitutional law, and only then after significant harm has been done by the offending statute. The odds of review by the High Court are a long shot at best today.

Of approximately 7,000 applications for constitutional review each year, the Supreme Court hears roughly 70 of them. With such miserable odds of illegal legislation or bad lower court decisions being challenged in the Court, the Legislative Branch (and lower courts) have known little restraint.

In the case of the Executive Branch, it has neutralized the Supreme Court for all intents and purposes, while becoming imperial in manner, with no regard for law or the Constitution and the court has shown no stomach for challenging its master.

The result of this willful neglect and dereliction of duty by the Supreme Court has been the proliferation of laws repugnant to the Constitution, and the advent of an Executive-run police state, complete with kangaroo courts and professional prosecutors to enforce them. These courts are staffed almost exclusively by former prosecutors as their judges, which has been a recipe for disaster, making us the largest penal colony ever in mankind's history.

The 18,000+ police agencies that have mushroomed across post-constitutional America, employ hundreds of thousands of agents looking for (or creating) infractions of 14,000+ mostly illegitimate federal laws, on a daily basis. The unconstitutional and seriously misnomered Department of Justice now has 93 offices scattered around the United States, staffed to the gills with largely-unsupervised young lawyers seeking convictions, by using constitutionally repugnant statutes and methods, which would make a third-world despot blush.

77.1% of their victims will never be allowed a moment of freedom to prepare their defense, as the Eighth Amendment in the Bill of Rights requires. The courts have re-interpreted this inalienable right to be an elective one, rendering it no longer a right at all.

Since the ridiculously named Bail Reform Act of 1984, whose "reform" was to eliminate the right to bail in most federal cases, all these Executive Branch U.S. Attorneys have to do to have their targets trapped and illegally detained is to claim to the court that the citizen is a "flight risk" or "a danger to the community." Taking no chances on fairness, they claim both in almost every case I have reviewed.

The victim is then held interminably, outside of statutory law (The Speedy Trial Act of 1974) as well as the Sixth Amendment (the right to a Public and Speedy Trial), until there is no alternative other than to negotiate a plea of guilty to an often unconstitutional or uncommitted *crime* to end being illegally held in a dangerous and overcrowded county jail. It works, just like King George's Tower of London did in his day, but it is illegal.

The federal government has achieved a 98.6% conviction rate using these brutal and odious tactics, and filled every jail bed and most of their floor space across the nation with American citizens who have not been convicted by any court of law.

Having been a victim of this corrupt system, I speak from having suffered each of these wrongs personally, not hypothetically.

The Speedy Trial Act (18 U.S.C. §3161, et seq), is broken into sections. §3164(c) demands the release of these prisoners designated as "high risk" by the prosecutors if they are not tried within 90 days of arrest or arraignment. I never once saw or heard of this law being followed.

The definition of a "speedy trial" in §3161(c)(l) of the Act is 70 days. Federal law and the Constitution are violated if the prisoner is not tried within that time, plus any excludable delays. This has not happened in a single of the hundreds of cases I've reviewed, nor did it happen in my own.

§3162(a)(2) requires the indictment to be dismissed "upon motion of the defendant" if the 70-day clock is violated, but defendants are not advised of this right, and lawyers are now sanctioned in many U.S. District Courts for filing such a motion. Though I *did* know of this rule and ordered six attorneys to file such a motion, in writing, and wrote the federal judge directly regarding it, law was ignored by all and the indictment was not dismissed.

The National Association of Criminal Defense Lawyers estimated in 2009 that 75% of the prison population in America may have been wrongfully convicted largely due to the failure of government to follow law. From experience, it is also the attorneys' recalcitrance to force them to do so, that has combined to create this horrifying situation.

It is truly heartbreaking. When one considers that the laws under which these convicted citizens were charged were in areas over which federal government had no authority to begin with, it goes from heartbreaking to disgusting.

The Department of Justice, which has foisted this horror on the nation, was the invention of President Ulysses S. Grant and the Republican post-Civil War government that had not yet allowed the defeated southern States to re-enter the Union. The result of the founding of this department was to usurp much of the power of the federal Judiciary, greatly increase it, and put it under the control of the Executive Branch, where it remains to this day.[12]

The Department of Justice was officially created in March of 1870. This agency, un-recognized by the Constitution, was placed under the portfolio of Attorney General, Amos T. Akerman, who reported directly to the President of the United States in nothing short of a power play that would disrupt the balance and separation of powers. It has also allowed the political donors and corporations to direct the changes they wanted in government by force of law and influence politically motivated attacks on others. This has been done to our severe detriment.

There simply is no authorization in Article II of the U.S. Constitution empowering the Executive Branch to control such a department, and the statistics readily prove its true purpose. Nationally famous attorney, Harvey A. Silverglate, revealed the endemic corruption and abuse of power within this Executive Department in 2009, in his landmark book, *Three Felonies a Day: How the Feds Target the Innocent.*" (Encounter Books, NY). He cited a study which can only lead to one conclusion about the true purpose for this department, and its unauthorized inclusion as an Executive power:

"*Study by Professors Donald C. Shields and John F. Cragan found that between 2001 and 2007 the D.O.J. [Department of Justice] opened investigations into seven times more Democratic public officials than Republican. The professors concluded that the odds of this discrepancy being a random occurrence were one in ten thousand.*"

Recent revelations of the Obama Administration targeting Republican fund-raising organizations should prove that this

---

12 *While it is widely believed that the Department of Justice is under the purview of the Judicial branch of government, it is not. 28 U.S.C. §501* **Executive department,** *states: "The department of Justice is an executive department of the United States at the seat of Government." (Added Pub. L.89-554, §4(c), Sept. 6, 1966, 80 Stat.611.)*

Executive department is nothing more than a blunt political tool, abused by both parties. It is not one of justice, nor was it intended to be. It is also unconstitutional.

Prior to this departure from the U.S. Constitution, no prosecution could be brought against a citizen by any branch of federal government until it was reviewed by the Attorney General's office and confirmed to be under the purview of federal power and authority. Then, the party wishing to bring the charge was required to prove that sufficient evidence existed for a conviction, prior to a prosecution ever being initiated.

The purpose and result of this onerous procedure was to prevent false, malicious or politically-motivated attacks on citizens. It also acted as a component of the overall checks and balances of constitutional government. The citizens were the beneficiaries of those protections and they are the losers as a result of their disappearance under the Department of Justice's reign.

Prior to this unconstitutional tinkering by President Grant and his Reconstruction Congress, the Attorney General did not even head up an executive department. He was an advisor to the President, as well as representing the government as plaintiff or defendant in cases before the Supreme Court. The Attorney General and his 94 Offices of U.S. Attorneys (including his headquarters) can now target any person, political organization, or institution in America, and destroy them at will.

The results of creating this massive department with the power to prosecute and destroy, under the authority of the Executive Branch and its chief politician, have been disastrous for the nation. The balance and separation of powers have been disrupted, some might claim, fatally. The Department of Justice was the genesis of the police state that exists today.

The Supreme Court seems to have been oblivious to all of this. It did not ever challenge President Lincoln after he ignored its ruling in *Ex parte Merryman*, where it was decided that only

Congress had the power to suspend the privilege of *habeas corpus* (after Lincoln had done so unilaterally in 1861 by Executive Order One). Perhaps the justices feared being put back in the basement of Congress and chose handsome surroundings to doing their job. We'll never know.

But the timid tone was set. The Supreme Court has continued its timorous ways since then with one notable exception known as the "Switch in time that saved nine" scandal. That ended its independence as a branch of government for all intents and purposes in 1937, in my opinion. The Hughes Court was set to reject President Franklin Roosevelt's New Deal legislation as unconstitutional, which according to Article I, Section 8, it was. When Roosevelt threatened to liquidate the justices' voting power by increasing the number of justices on the court to 15, Justice Hughes folded opposition and capitulated to the powerful president. Article III does not specifically state that there must be nine judges on the Supreme Court, so Roosevelt's threat was very real. His additional judges would undoubtedly have been confirmed by his party which controlled Congress.

It is high time, however, for the Judicial Branch to reestablish itself. Article III does not require or even contemplate Supreme Court Justices being attorneys. Many of our greatest justices and leaders have not been formally trained in law, including its Fourth Chief Justice, John Marshall, and the main author of the Constitution, James Madison.[13] The sole purpose of the Supreme Court is to keep the nation within the boundaries of the Constitution. This is not a job which requires a law degree, obviously, as *its author did not have one*. It is a job for sensible people who have studied our Founders' intent and care about their nation and

---

13 *While Gouverneur Morris, John Blair, and Thomas Jefferson (via correspondence from his duties in France) did have legal training and great input into the content and wording of the U.S. Constitution, James Madison, a non-lawyer, is recognized as its principle author*

its freedom. James Madison's words are extraordinarily simple and clear.

The system today has become so perverted under the custody and care of lawyers and politicians that it is unrecognizable as American justice. An excellent example is the outrageous Reagan-era conspiracy laws passed, ostensibly, as a temporary measure to be used against Mafia bosses. These terrifying laws are now used in 90% of all federal cases. There is no defense against a charge of conspiracy, which is why the Department of Justice now uses it in almost every case. Civilized nations do not have such laws due to their potential for abuse.

Conspiracy is an inchoate crime of thought. It is not the commission of a crime, it is thinking about one. No overt act is required in order to be guilty and any two immunity hunters, known or unknown to government's target(s), can say that their fellow citizen *thought* about committing a crime and he or she will face more time in prison in many cases, than if they had committed the crime itself.

While sentences for murder, rape, robbery and aggravated assault, real crimes, now average 49 months, a conviction for the vague crime of thought–*conspiracy*–is often for decades. Our nation must rid itself of these tool of unrestrained abuse by prosecutors immediately.

Even the nation's closest neighbors, Canada and The Bahamas, refuse to extradite any citizen, even an American, if conspiracy is the charge, as it is an immoral and indefensible law, which is unconstitutionally vague. No one can know it is being violated, nor can the defendant prove innocence.

This entire process has deteriorated from beginning to end under the Department of Justice and the political hacks who run it. The ancient grand jury process, which was created to protect the citizen from wrongful prosecution, has been transformed into a secretive affair which all but insures it. Sinister deeds and evil in every shape have full swing there today.

Targets of these inquisitions are no longer allowed to have an attorney. False evidence and compensated witnesses scripted to lie by government prosecutors are presented with impunity and transcripts are not allowed their victims where those misdeeds and their misconduct can be exposed. The targets of these illegitimate courts are often not allowed to be present themselves to raise a defense or contest government's fabrications.

In today's Department of Justice system, this grand jury *show* is the closest 95% of government's victims will ever get to a trial though the Sixth Amendment still requires all criminal defendants "the right to a speedy and public trial, by an impartial jury of the State and district where-in the crime shall have been committed." Today's grand jury is a rubber stamp affair where it said that a prosecutor can "indict a ham sandwich."

19 out of 20 of federal government's victims will be forced to take a plea agreement via extortion, threats, intimidation and/or incarceration of their loved ones. These coerced agreements are binding on the citizen but not on government, and in my considerable experience as both a victim and reviewer, I have never seen the federal government keep a single bargain it made to lure the citizen into signing away years of his or her life.

Since 1967, prosecutors and judges who commit these crimes against **We the People**, are immune from prosecution for their own violations of law and Constitution. They are above the law, by law, which is itself a violation of the Equal Treatment Clause (Amendment Fourteen). This came about due to a string of court decisions beginning with *Pierson v. Ray* in 1967, not by legislation. In other words, the courts granted themselves and their prosecutors immunity. Judges and prosecutors *suffer no penalty for violating the law and rights of* **We the People** *while performing their duties in our name.* Until this changes, they will continue to break the law with impunity. Thomas Jefferson once again warned of this happening:

"The Judiciary of the United States is the subtle corps of sappers and miners constantly working under ground to undermine the foundations of our confederated fabric." (1820)

"...the Federal Judiciary; an irresponsible body (for impeachment is only a scarecrow), working like gravity by night and day, gaining a little to-day and a little tomorrow, and advancing its noiseless step like a thief, over the field of jurisdictions, until all shall be usurped from the States, and the government of all be consolidated into one...." (1821)

Historians and constitutional scholars need to be on the Supreme Court in balance with lawyers to prevent further lawlessness by the High Court itself. Allowing judges and prosecutors to continue escaping punishment for the violation of constitutional rights, is a crime in itself. Non-lawyer jurists and justices would stop such constitutional anomalies, rather than ignoring them.

Jefferson's prophecy has come to pass. The oppression of the U.S. government and its federal judiciary are far worse than any ever beheld under King George III of England. America's prison population stands in evidence. Jefferson would be shocked and dismayed, however, that the federal judiciary has allowed its powers to be usurped and absorbed by what he intended to be the weakest arm of government, the Executive branch. It is the presidency, in the end, which has exacerbated our run to tyranny, using the judiciary as little more than a tool to do it.

The final insult and injury to **We the People** in the judicial arena has been the virtual elimination of jury powers, which under the Constitution are *unlimited*. These awesome powers still exist, but judges at all levels often tell juries the opposite in their instructions.

American citizens are no longer taught their rights in government schools and few take the time to learn them. The credit for the corrosive tactic of failing to inform jurors of their rights falls to the judges, but guilt must be shared by sycophantic lawyers and Congress, who have allowed the foul practice to go unchallenged.

A decision made by a jury is unreviewable, for any reason. This ultimate power was retained by *We the People* as a safeguard against the tyranny we now face, but not knowing of it makes this power meaningless and of no value to anyone. A juror in a trial is more powerful than any judge, legislator, or even the President.

Jurors are also the real judges in constitutional courts and the judges on the bench are just referees. Jurors have the right, power, and duty to judge not only the facts in the case, *but whether the law itself is valid or not.* The only power a judge has over a juror is that person's ignorance about his or her own unlimited authority. The judgment of a jury is above question or challenge by the court.

This is an important part of the foundation of the balance of powers as well as the legislators' best means of feedback from *We the People* when unacceptable laws are passed. If juries refuse to convict defendants under a certain law, which is called *jury nullification*, it sends a message to Congress or the legislature that it has erred by passing it.

Judges and government are powerless to do anything about such decisions, and have taken the odious route of lying to the jurors about their power over recent decades, to prevent lawful *nullification.* The mere mention of jury rights in a courtroom today will earn a lawyer a citation for contempt of court. Such courts are contemptible, as the law is clear:

"The jury has an unreviewable and unreversible power.... to acquit in disregard of the instructions on the law given by a trial judge." U.S. v. Dougherty, 473 F 2d 1113, 1139 (1972)

Refusing to convict citizens under bad or unconstitutional law sends a clear message to the legislators that they have gone too far. It was this process of jury nullification which has been credited for causing the repeal of unconstitutional legislation such as The Alien and Sedition Acts (1798), The Fugitive Slave Act (1850), and other blights on the American conscience. It will hopefully save the nation from the *conspiracy* laws one day, once jurors again know of their powers to nullify repugnant laws by refusing to convict their fellow citizens who are attacked under them.

Judicial instructions to the jury, as recently as my own teen-age years accompanying my attorney grandfather, H. Osler Woltz, Sr., to court, still included the right to nullify, so these despicable changes are quite recent.

Judge Peter Hairston's jury instructions in the Surry County courthouse of North Carolina in the 1960s were as follows:

"It is not only your power to decide the facts in this case, but to rule on the law itself. If it is not in keeping with your own conscience, you values, or those of your community, it is within your power to set this man free."

In Maryland, as recently as the 1980s, juries were advised by judges, that they were not required to follow judicial instructions. In a 1967 jury instruction from a murder trial recently in the news, the judge stated, *"You, under our system, in criminal cases are at liberty to disagree with the court's interpretation of the law. You shall determine what the law is and then apply the law to the facts as you find them to be."*

Such honest instructions must return to the courtrooms of the United States. Jury nullification is the ultimate check and balance on government abuse of power. The Judicial Branch was to be controlled by *We the People* and our juries, not the government. That control must return to us. The judicial powers of prosecution at the federal level must be wrested from the President and his U.S. Attorneys. Open, fair, grand juries, under the control of *We the People* is where that power constitutionally belongs. The courts are the People's venue and their protection against government, not a tool for the President or his political minions to oppress and imprison them.

ACTION PLAN

STEP 1- Establish Supreme Court preview of all congressional legislation for compliance with the U.S. Constitution prior to enactment, as a safeguard against further trespass into areas outside of constitutionally listed federal powers.

STEP 2- End Executive branch authority over the Department of Justice immediately. No such power is granted under Article II of the Constitution and Congress had no power under Article I, Section 8 to create it as a department or added purview of the Executive Branch.

STEP 3- End federal prosecutions for violations of laws which are not specifically authorized by the United States Constitution as a function of federal government to enforce.

STEP 4- Close the 93 United States Attorney's Offices around the United States and return to the constitutional practice of justifying a federal prosecution prior to its initiation. The federal courts were never intended to be used for criminal prosecutions. Other than piracy on the high seas and against the laws of other nations; or counterfeiting federal securities and money, such criminal justice was to be the purview of the States.*

STEP 5- Restore the sanctity of the venerable grand jury process where it is open, public, and no citizen can be indicted without having the opportunity to present his or her side, confront government's witnesses, and be represented by an attorney. There is no place for secrecy in the American judicial process and no legal excuse for it.

STEP 6- Require jury rights and the power of nullification to be part of every instruction given by the courts at both State and federal levels. (See Note below)

STEP 7- Start grassroots movement to pressure Presidential candidates to put constitutional scholars and historians on the Supreme Court, to balance the corrosive effect the legal profession has had on that institution. James Madison was not an attorney, and one is not required to interpret his words.

* Treason is also the province of the federal Courts, but it is listed under Article III as a power of the Judiciary to control. Congress's power to declare its punishment is granted as a federal power under Article III, Section 3 (Judicial Powers), but not the authority to implement laws regarding it.

Note- The State of New Hampshire passed legislation in 2012 that explicitly allowed lawyers to tell juries about their power of nullification, which had previously been unlawfully banned by the courts. While an exciting return to law and recognition of a jury's true powers, this bill has not had the desired effect, possibly due to attorneys' fear of retaliation by judges and prosecutors. A second bill has been introduced in the New Hampshire legislature which "would require judges to tell juries in every criminal case that they are free to exercise a long-standing but controversial power called 'nullification," according to The Wall Street Journal (January 22, 2014, *Another Path to 'Not Guilty'*). This is a beginning, and hopefully, every other State will follow suit.

RESTORING THE MILITARY TO CONSTITUTIONAL BOUNDARIES

The United States military is a difficult subject to address. Americans have been trained by government from birth to stand and sing martial tunes and revere battle. Any question regarding the scope and size of the nation's vast military presence around the globe is considered tantamount to treason.

But this book is about truth and what the United States was meant to be, not the propaganda we've been taught by the government and those who control it.

The author of the Constitution, James Madison, considered *a standing army* such as we now have, to be the most dangerous threat to liberty possible. The author of the Declaration of Independence, Thomas Jefferson, considered it second only to the dangers of a central bank.

We now have both.

Madison wrote:

"Of all the enemies to public liberty war is, perhaps, the most to be dreaded because it comprises and develops the germ of every other. War is the parent of armies; from these proceed debt and taxes.... known instruments for bringing the many under the domination of the few.... No nation could preserve its freedom in the midst of continual warfare."

Since the end of World War II, the United States has fought over 170 engagements. The nation has been in a state of continual warfare, some public, many in secret, all undeclared, though that is demanded by the U.S. Constitution. Every one of these wars was illegal under our Constitution.

The United States military now has 170 publicly known bases and operations scattered around the world and many more secret ones, some of which have only recently been identified. The U.S. still has troops from World War II stationed across Europe and Asia, and over 30,000 soldiers remain in Korea, from a conflict which ended in 1954.

U.S. forces lost over 2,000 planes and five battleships in that war, with over two million casualties and deaths on both sides, but "war" was never declared, rendering it illegal.

America's military spending for 2009 was $1.067 trillion.[14] The rest of the world, combined, spent approximately $438 billion.

Our enemy of the month, Communist China, increased military spending to just $57.8 billion in 2009 and the U.S. media and State Department howled of "dangerous escalation." The Republic of China, with 4.6 times the population of the U.S., spends 1/18 or 5.5% as much on defense. The Chinese government spends its revenues building its nation, as ours should be doing. Our leaders now spend our revenues destroying others to enrich the war industry and its suppliers, while our infrastructure crumbles. That is not only stupid, it is unconstitutional. Our forces are to be defensive in nature, not offensive.

The most conservative comparison of U.S. military spending I can find (The Economist, 02/19/2011, p. 14) places it "currently equivalent to that of the next 20 countries combined."

Even the most ardent hawk must see that such wasteful spending and excessive pandering to the military-industrial complex has little, if anything, to do with *defense*.

---

14 *This figure included the cost of the troop "surge", excess requests for the wars in Iraq and Afghanistan, as well as new weapons programs*

The only beneficiaries of war are those who supply it and those who finance it. Those are the same entities and corporations that now control our representatives in Congress or this could not have happened. When is enough, enough?

The nation's first president, George Washington, warned in his Farewell Address to stay out of foreign affairs and instead, "Observe good faith and justice towards all nations; cultivate peace and harmony with all." Our leaders have refused George Washington's advice and stay in a state of perpetual war. As James Madison pointed out, "No nation could preserve its freedom in the midst of continual warfare," and we have not.

The United States, under corporate control, has caused this. It is time to get back to the basics of the Founders' intent.

The proper and only role of the American military is as a defensive force, *in time of declared war.* The only national force authorized to exist in times of peace is the United States Navy, which is designated to protect the nation's coasts and keep sea lanes open for commercial traffic. Article I, Section 8 is clear. Federal government is "To provide *and maintain* a Navy."

In time of declared war–and only then–Congress is authorized "To raise and support Armies, but no Appropriation of Money to that Use shall be for a longer Term than two years."

A standing federal army, when no war has been declared, was and is unconstitutional, plain and simple. One can be raised in time of declared war, but no standing army is allowed in time of peace, other than State Militias. That does not mean that the nation was to be defenseless. Our Founders styled their military land forces after the most successful defense force in human history, the Swiss Army. The Swiss model had already kept that nation out of war for hundreds of years in the 1770s and 1780s when Madison, Washington and Jefferson were planning our military, and it has ever since. That is still our nation's model by law and constitution, and the means by which George

Washington was able to defeat the greatest army on earth during the Revolutionary War.

The Swiss Army has successfully defended its nation since the 1500s, despite Europe being a battlefield all around it for most of that period of history. The Swiss Confederation has successfully maintained its neutrality and peace for half a millennia, and has the highest per capita standard of living in the world because of it. *"War is the parent of armies; from these proceed debt and taxes...,"* as James Madison warned.

Swiss leadership is under a triumvirate, as Benjamin Franklin wanted for the United States presidency. The Swiss have not squandered their nation's wealth on war as U.S. presidents have squandered ours. U.S. leaders left the constitutional Swiss model over a century ago, and have since bankrupted the nation with their standing army and continuous warfare.

The expenditures wasted on corporate-sponsored war for the past fiscal *year* would have funded a *constitutional* military for most, if not all, of our nation's history.

A *constitutional* army is very inexpensive and has but one purpose, which is to protect and preserve the independence of the nation. The Swiss model on which our Founders based our own was and is based on a system of universal cantonal conscription under which every Swiss male is expected to serve as a member of his Canton's (State) military between 20 and 42 years of age. Officers serve until the age of 52. This is the *constitutional* method of State militias as described in Article I, Section 8.

Initial training is followed by 10 three-week refresher courses. Swiss females also serve on a volunteer basis in the women's military force. The nation's people are its army.

Swiss soldiers keep their weapons, ammunition and equipment in their homes and are ready to deploy at a moment's notice. Gunnery practice is obligatory each year and it is performed in civilian clothes.

This model of military develops and maintains an extraordinary degree of trust between government and its citizens *as it was designed to do.* In our model, the States were to control the land forces for their protection (internal) and the federal government was to control the navy to protect the coast (external) and sea lanes. That is still our *constitutional military model.*

A federal government whose army is its own private citizenry, under State or cantonal controlled military units, cannot abuse them or violate that trust except at its own peril. It also cannot subject them to the tyranny of corporate interests to their own detriment as our federal government has done.

That seems to be the only logical explanation for the United States government to have so flagrantly violated the U.S. Constitution and created its standing armies. The corporate interests needed aggressive mercenary assault forces, not defensive ones. The resulting military-industrial complex wanted a perpetual war machine, to keep profits high, and that is what they got, thanks to their ability to purchase the representatives of *We the People.*

The last time the United States of America was attacked by a foreign army was in 1812. A constitutional American army defeated the British Army—the most powerful in the world—so soundly that neither they nor anyone else has ever tried since.

As the Swiss and United States have proven, no standing army of mercenaries is a match for well-trained citizen-warriors protecting their homes.

No army wants to go door-to-door against the Swiss and none has ever tried, including Napoleon or Hitler, though they controlled all nations around them. Trained citizen-warriors defending their homes are worth ten conscripted soldiers. Even the brief Swiss alliance of its French-speaking cantons with Napoleon was not a war, and lasted only briefly.[15]

---

15 *The French-speaking cantons of the Swiss confederation were lured into an alliance with Napoleon in 1798 and created the Helvetic Republic. By 1803, they rejoined the*

The camaraderie and sense of community built by regional defense forces are anathema to federalism and strong central government. They do not serve corporate America either, which is why Congress and the Executive Branch have created an unconstitutional federal standing army to replace them, in my opinion. It is time for this constitutional anomaly to end before it destroys our nation. Let the corporations hire their own army.

The land forces must revert to State-controlled and managed military units, to be called upon by federal government, only in time of a defensive war, officially declared by Congress.

Military bases and National Guard posts located in each State could easily revert to local control and scale down to be defensive in nature rather than offensive as they are today. If anything, local soldiers, living at their homes in that State, ready to defend it or the nation, is a far greater *defense and deterrent* to outside hostilities than any other, while causing no hatred abroad.

Any needed foreign intelligence would be the responsibility of the United States Navy, the nation's external force. A nation engaging in "Peace, commerce, and honest friendship with all nations — entangling alliances with none," as Thomas Jefferson advocated, has no need of further intelligence capabilities or a standing army.

How others choose to live is their own affair unless they encroach on our soil or our people, which is very unlikely in a peaceful nation that minds its own business as the Swiss have proven for half a millennia. Should any nation make such a terrible mistake as to attack them (or us), they would think they stepped into a hornet's nest.

All military power (external) must revert to the control of the U.S. Congress. Internal and land-based forces must return to the control of the States. The U.S. President has no authority over either except in time of declared war, at which time he becomes Commander and Chief for the duration of the conflict only.

Republic to make the original 13 cantons. Six new cantons later joined to form the 19 canton Helvetic Confederation as it exists today

Americans must honestly ask themselves whom war really serves. War does not serve the young men and women who die in them before they've had an opportunity to taste life. It does not serve their parents and loved ones who lose them, and in fact, it does them great harm.

Invading foreign nations, even with good intentions, is rarely a service in the long run. It is not our place, constitutionally, to force our way of life on anyone at the point of a gun anyway, though good intentions have rarely had anything to do with invasions by the United States, once the truth became known. Recent wars served other interests.

America's current wars like those of the past century of wars were sold to the nation with lies. Public sentiment was played upon by politicians and hyped by the corporate media. In the end, the only beneficiaries were the suppliers of war toys and services; and the bankers who financed them.

Six hundred thousand Iraqis are dead at our nation's hands, to extricate the puppet, Saddam Hussein, whom our own government put in place there years ago. The infrastructure of their nation has been obliterated by our standing army and one of every forty of its people is now dead.

Forty percent of the soldiers sent by our nation's politicians to fight these wars for corporate resources are returning home with mental problems, which is only natural. No sane person can be told to invade and murder innocent people and destroy their country without having psychological difficulties from so doing, or be psychotic to the point that it has no effect on them.

The United States Constitution does not allow this kind of activity and it must stop now. Foreign bases must close, except those necessary to keep the nation's navy repaired and fueled. No nation has need of 170+ bases around the world, with troops ready to invade foreign lands, if it is a free and peaceful country as ours was meant to be.

Those young men and women need to be brought home to help rebuild our own nation; a constitutional America.

ACTION PLAN

STEP 1- Congress must reassert its authority over the military forces and remove any Executive Branch control, except in time of declared war.

STEP 2- Federal land-based forces must devolve to State control as required by the United States Constitution. Congress may prescribe their training regimen and call them to service in time of declared war, but they are the responsibility, and under the control of, the respective States between those declared wars.

STEP 3- Foreign U.S. military presence other than is necessary to keep sea lanes open for commercial traffic and gather intelligence under the U.S. Navy must end.

PUTTING THE CORPORATE GENIE BACK IN THE BOTTLE

The common denominator of our national ills from uncontrollable pollution and unnecessary wars, to bloated federal government and our loss of freedom can be found in the corporate powers that control the federal government today. I am not discussing small companies, but the giants.

International corporations are now the dominant cultural and economic force on earth and directly or indirectly control the planet's stores of natural resources. The transnational corporate giants hold combined assets valued at more than the total worth of over half the nations of the world. They also control most of its governments, directly or indirectly, and write most of those nations' legislation and laws. This has acted to neutralize national governments as a safeguard against corporations and their misdeeds.

Big corporations survive and thrive only in an environment of big governments and world powers. Theirs is a symbiotic relationship.

The huge sums of money these corporations dangle before politicians the world over in such dizzying amounts would tempt the most chaste and honest of men. Those are characteristics rarely associated with politicians and to that temptation, they have proven themselves quite vulnerable.

Legislation is bought and sold as if in a market and the loser is always *We the People*. This prostitution of power and money must come to an end.

Adam Smith, the father of capitalist theory according to most economists, is the man many of these huge corporate entities would no doubt consider as their patron saint. What these oligarchs practice, however, is as far from Smith's capitalism as its opposing economic theories, such as communism. Adam Smith warned of this back in 1776 and described corporations and "joint stock companies" as they were commonly called in his day, "nuisances in every respect."[16] Smith claimed that they "have in the long run proved, universally, either burdensome or useless, and have either mismanaged or confined the trade."[17] Smith wrote:

"The usual corporate spirit, wherever the law does not restrain it, prevails in all regulated companies. When they have been allowed to act according to their own natural genius, they have always, in order to confine the competition to as small a number as possible, endeavoured to subject the trade to many burdensome regulations." [18]

This process of kicking away the ladder after climbing to the top unrestrained, has worked well for large American corporations and professions such as law and medicine. "Burdensome regulations" only benefit those already well-established in the industry or profession, by making entry of new competitors increasingly difficult if not impossible, thereby protecting those already in it from true capitalism and competition. Big corporate interests need big government to employ the law to protect them from competition by would-be entrants into the industry and professions to which they seek to limit entry. Regulation and red-tape worked in Adam

---

16 *Smith, Adam. An Inquiry into the Nature and Causes of the Wealth of Nations. Vol. 36, Chronology of Great Authors, Encyclopaedia BrittanicaInc., Chicago, IL, Sixth Edition, 1996, p.313*

17 *Ibid.*

18 *Ibid.*

Smith's day, and they do today, keeping small companies out of the marketplace, and professionals limited in numbers, by their own private monopolies.

Smith described the corporate power over the law-making process as "like an overgrown standing army, they have become formidable to the government and upon many occasions intimidate the legislature." [19]

Those legislators who support every proposal for the corporate interests and monopolists, Smith stated enjoy "great popularity and influence with an order of men whose numbers and wealth render them of great importance." Of those who oppose them, Adam Smith wrote "neither the highest rank, nor the greatest public services can protect him from the most infamous abuse and detraction, from personal insults, nor sometimes from real danger, arising from the insolent outrage of furious and disappointed monopolists." [20]

The father of capitalism was relentless in his attacks on these market distorting anomalies known as "corporations" and "joint-stock companies." He listed 55 of their failures from his day in *The Wealth of Nations*, to make his point. Perhaps Smith's greatest insult was when he wrote, "they are certainly altogether useless. To be merely useless is perhaps the highest eulogy which could ever justly be bestowed upon a regulated company."[21]

Big corporate America would be far better suited with Ghengis Khan or Attila the Hun as its patron saint rather than Adam Smith. Companies were his sworn enemy, and what they do today in America is not Adam Smith's capitalism, it is government-sanctioned oligarchy. From the Virginia Company land corporation, which established the colony in Jamestown in 1606, and

---

19 *Ibid.*

20 *Ibid.*

21 *Ibid.*

the Plymouth Company (also chartered in 1606) destined for Massachusetts, the corporate virus was transplanted to America. It has gone from a mere nuisance like a common cold, to life threatening in its virulent present-day form.

Corporate charters were only granted for purposes that could be claimed to be in some public interest for most of our history. Charters were granted to corporations for expanding ports, building bridges and importing certain goods that were needed but not available in the colonies. Public service had to be a component of a corporation's reason for being. Corporate charters were granted for a fixed-time only.

The canal-building era, which began in 1817 when the State of New York chartered a privately-owned corporation to build the 363 mile Erie Canal between Lake Erie and the Hudson River, was a turning point. Such public service corporations were chartered then for as few as ten years, and only while they performed the service for which they were created. The corporation and its charter then expired, and any remaining business became a non-corporate proprietorship, without any special protections or privileges from government.

This was the marketplace where Adam Smith's theories that people "are led by an invisible hand to make nearly the same distribution of the necessaries of life," and true capitalism thrived and actually benefited the public as well as the proprietor. All corporations in our nation's early history were held to such standards. No State would authorize one to exist unless it served a public need and corporations were not allowed to buy one another or keep monopolistic powers. Failure to fulfill their purpose, or to carry out the proposed public service or fiduciary duty, was also a cause for charter revocation.

This system survived for roughly a century before the advent of the Golden Era of the Robber Barons of the railroads, which changed it forever. Private corporations were given land grants of over 130 million acres from the humble beginnings of the Baltimore and Ohio Railroad in 1830 up through the completion of the transcontinental line in 1869 when the Central Pacific connected to the Union Pacific in Promontory, Utah. These government grants were the foundations of some of the vast fortunes which would soon control the nation's political process.

From Andrew Carnegie's first fortune earned selling railroad bonds, through the oligarchs Cornelius Vanderbilt (New York Central Railroad), James Hill (Northern Pacific), Leland Stanford (Central Pacific), E. Henry Harriman (Union Pacific), Collis Huntington (Southern Pacific), and on to J.P. Morgan himself, the die was cast.

The crowning blow of granting citizenship to these bodiless entities in 1886 (*Santa Clara County v. Southern Pacific Railroad*), gave these men the means to buy control of the nation, with fortunes granted them by the government of that nation, through their *public service* monopolies.

Once corporations were legally able to bribe politicians using their status as *citizens* after the unconstitutional decision in *Santa Clara County*, the United States government became a tool in their service rather than a limiting or restraining factor on them, just as Abraham Lincoln had predicted.

Big corporations and big government were soul mates. They thrived together, sucking the nation and its people dry, while creating the great disparity we see today between rich and poor; the powerful and the powerless.

The United States went from the most free and prosperous nation on earth, to a bankrupt police state owing $68 trillion, which it can never repay. $54 trillion of that debt (borrowed from Social Security) is to **We the People**, but it is unlikely we will ever see it. The rest is owed largely to foreign nations and banks, and is growing at nearly $2 trillion each year as the corporatocracy digs us ever deeper into insolvency and tyranny.

The question is not whether to stop them or not, but whether or not there is time left to do so. Between their continued stripping of our planet of all its natural resources, and their constant wars to secure them, we simply may not survive long enough to break their iron grip on our nation, its politicians, or our world.

The first step is to wrest control of Congress from the corporations as laid out in Step One, but more must be done to break their means of ever controlling our nation again.

It was not until the States of New Jersey and Delaware were coerced into relaxing their laws regarding corporations at the behest (and cash) of John D. Rockefeller and J.P. Morgan that the corporate genie was completely out of the bottle, and this is where we must turn to put him back in it. These *enabling acts* were sold to the States as means of generating revenues. Once adopted by Delaware and New Jersey, the race to the bottom was on. Other States quickly followed suit and corporations were given incredible power and rights, while being concurrently relieved of any attendant responsibilities.

Public service was no longer required and true ownership could be occluded from public view in some States, as is still the case in Delaware and Nevada today. Freed of public service requirements, and protected by the corporate veil of liability, the nation was the corporations' oyster. Politicians have been bought and sold like livestock ever since, to do their bidding.

The next stage of restoration is therefore at this State level where the problem began and where corporations are still formed and regulated. These entities must be limited once more in their use, scope and boundaries. Each State should prescribe, by law, what it demands of any corporation, be it one of their own or from another state or nation, before it can operate (or continue to operate) within that State. There should once again be a requirement of public service and need, otherwise, businesses should remain proprietorships or limited affairs, which would keep them on a human scale, unable to control governments and the political process.

There will be court battles and lawsuits aplenty, and it will not be an easy task, but the States must re-assert their power to control what goes on in their sovereign jurisdictions, to break the hegemony of the national and transnational corporations over this nation, if not the world.

Corporations have no sovereignty. Nothing in the United States Constitution justifies the outrageous decision in *Santa Clara County v. Southern Pacific Railroad* granting citizenship rights to a box of papers and a corporate seal back in 1886. The history of how these oligarchs contrived this Supreme Court decision should itself be cause for its overturn, as well as all of the subsequent decisions based on it, but that is another story.

There simply is no legal basis for corporate citizenship, period. The word *corporation* is not mentioned in the United States Constitution, and that contract is with **We the People, not Them the Corporations.**

American jurisprudence holds that an unconstitutional statute or judicial decision, though having the name and form of law, is wholly void and ineffective for any purpose.

"An unconstitutional act is not law; it confers no rights; it imposes no duties; affords no protection; it creates no office; it is in legal contemplation, as inoperative as though it had never been passed." (*Norton v. Shelby County*, 118 US 425, p.442)

"No one is bound to obey an unconstitutional law and no courts are bound to enforce it."(16 AmJur 2d,§177, late 2d,§256)

The Supreme Court cannot (legally) create words not found in the U.S. Constitution, nor can it confer rights not authorized by it. The day of corporate rule over the United States (and its High Court) must draw to a close soon or our nation is lost to them forever.

This effort can begin at the State level by re-establishing the principles upon which corporations were originally allowed to be formed–public service. Unless a public service can be established and fulfilled by that corporation, and that State's criterion for formation can be met, the corporation should face dissolution or be barred from operation within that State's boundaries.

State law and requirements of resident ownership or board control could be applied to any corporation doing business within the State, ending the hegemony of a handful of retail giants. This would, simultaneously, act to restore local trade, local traders and local suppliers.

Capital would once more remain in the State and local banks and communities to fund and finance regional industries and diverse projects of local need and small businesses, rather than shifting to and pooling in the corporate capitals of the world, to fund transnationals operating elsewhere.

Local entrepreneurs, small business, and regional banks, could again fluoresce and build real, interdependent communities, putting an end to one-mill towns that dry up when the non-resident owners find cheaper labor elsewhere. The big-box stores, brands and chains, which do not serve any real public function, could be required to divest to local ownership or be replaced with a flourishing local economy of trade and commerce by individual proprietorships. Local products, produce and supplies would supplant the foreign made and grown, and revenues would remain within the community.

Business ownership and control over our lives and our communities would return to a human, local scale and scope, ending the rule of the corporate oligarchs from afar.

Non-resident corporate giants could no longer soil our rivers, lakes, shores and earth, protected by politicians from Washington, while leaving their mess and poisons behind them when they pull up stakes and slip away in the middle of the night for those who live there to suffer and repair.

A restored sense of community and common purpose would settle upon the land, as was once the case in America. The rich and diverse patchwork of regional cultures and life-styles that once existed could again revive and flourish.

This is not utopic thinking or dreaming, it is how it once was in America. In the years before the corporate takeover of the nation, foreign visitors such as the eloquent Alexis de Tocqueville, were amazed by what they saw.[22] He wrote of people living lives of such vitality in extraordinary freedom and peace that was unknown in Europe. Life with no masters or monarchs where man existed in an egalitarian society of unadulterated liberty was something so foreign to the rest of what de Tocqueville called the "modern world", that it was looked on with wonder and envy by the masses, and feared by the rulers and oligarchs in Europe.

There is no question that there were horrible injustices and unforgivable wrongs done by the rich and powerful in that day as well. The scourge of slavery in parts of the nation and mistreatment of those forced into that foul institution by federal government and the oligarchs of that day will be a perpetual stain on the nation's honor and psyche. Federal government both instituted and allowed this horrible circumstance, but it also had a hand in its undoing. Correcting injustices is a valid duty of federal government. Instituting them is not.

The 130 million acres federal government gave away to the Robber Barons of the 1800s were each stolen by that same federal government from the indigenous people who had lived on this land for what we now know to have been tens of thousands of years. In fact, the whole nation was pilfered from these people who had built their own societies of amazing grandeur before Hernando DeSoto and the swine that accompanied him in 1539, delivered the poxes that would decimate them.

There is no way to adequately recompense the Africans who labored under slavery to build the nation, or the native Americans

---

22 *As recorded in de Tocqueville's classic, Democracy in America*

whose lands were stolen and upon which it was built, except by creating a fair and free society wherein their descendants can again flourish and prosper.

The concepts of human freedom and egalitarianism were not brought to these shores by the European invaders. They were found here upon their arrival. The Founders marveled in their writings at the proud American Indian who knew no master and followed no leader except by his own choice. What Rousseau and Locke wrote about had been a way of life for centuries in America, but was yet unknown in most of Europe.

Returning to a just and free society where no man (or corporation) controls another, would be a small but due token to both the African American and the Native American.

From the Virginia Company, which murdered the Powhatans who had saved the Jamestown colonists, through the railroad corporations that bribed the federal government to steal the native's lands by force of arms, the corporations were second only to smallpox as the Indian's worst and fiercest enemy.

From the federally-sanctioned slave importation monopolies of the 1700s to the federal protection of strike-busters under color of law, the African-American and all oppressed parts of society can hail corporate America as their foe and a great source of their misery.

Corporate power now controls both of our nation's political parties, leaving little hope for change unless they can no longer fund candidates, as suggested in Step One. Our First Founding Father, George Washington, warned against these "parties" and loyalty to them rather than the nation. In his *Farewell Address*, Washington said that while parties may serve well "in governments of a monarchical cast," by encouraging the spirit of liberty, "in governments purely elective, it is a spirit not to be encouraged."

Corporations have bribed their way out of the requirement of public servitude, taken control of our political parties, and shed all responsibilities to the public. The huge corporations are no longer just "useless" and a "nuisance" as they were in the 1700s when Adam Smith wrote about them; they are now dangerous, virulent, and a threat to our nation's solvency and world stability.

This danger of transnational and mega-corporations controlling our own government and representatives, must be addressed forthwith as a prerequisite to finding our way back to a constitutional America.

ACTION PLAN

STEP 1- Begin the corporate reformation at State government level by revamping rules of incorporation on a state-by-state basis. Return requirement of public service to the granting of public charters (for large stock issuing companies doing business across State borders), and make them for a fixed time, dependent upon continued service and good behavior in that State, or refuse renewal.

STEP 2- Establish strict rules by which any corporation must abide in order to be allowed to incorporate or operate within the State. Some suggestions might include:

A. Corporations cannot directly or indirectly make contributions of any kind to political candidates, forums, PACs or even political parties.

B. Corporations engaged in any potentially harmful activity which may damage the environment must post a surety bond at maximum foreseeable cost of reparation, and shareholders must sign personal, non-waivable guarantees to cover any overage.

C. Corporations from other States with operations, outlets, offices or any presence within the State must comply with all State rules which should require local board members, management with authority to override non-local decision making, ownership; or suffer closure. Local control must be re-asserted. Non-compliant corporations from other States and nations might choose to sell local operations or franchises to State residents, but their national hegemony needs to be broken. The concept of free and open trade between the States applied to merchandise not matters of control and how they operated within those States.

STEP 10

THE SUSTAINABLE
WAY FORWARD

Hernando DeSoto landed in present-day Tampa Bay, Florida in 1539. He wrote in his journal of a land filled with people and areas of civilization which could not fit another dwelling. He and his 600 men traveled up through the present-day Carolinas and Tennessee, then south and west to the Mississippi River. DeSoto described a settled country and peaceful people with a meticulously cultivated landscape, where man lived in unison with nature.

What DeSoto did not know was that the swine, horses and soldiers comprising his expedition were delivering a death warrant to those settled, peaceful people. Recent estimates by researcher Charles C. Mann, in his 2005 book, 1491: *New Revelations of the Americas Before Columbus*, (Knopf Publishing, New York) place the death-toll of the indigenous people of North and Central America as high as 97% from these unknown European poxes and plagues. The invaders' immunity to them had taken centuries to develop, but the natives in America, were defenseless against them. It was the most horrific die-off of human kind in known history.

The British invaders, just 70 years later, found an empty landscape, hardly populated, with entire villages intact but devoid of a living soul. All that remained of the great cultures that had existed for tens of thousands of years were a handful of native Americans with their deep respect for Mother Earth, upon whose back they lived lightly; and the fierce sense of independence and love of liberty with which they would infect the invaders, leading ulti-mately to the severance of their ties with England in 1776.

But like the corporations of today, the invaders took the good without any of the responsibility attending it. They accepted the freedom aspect of the native culture, without the deep commit-ment and attendant responsibility to care for Mother Earth, which accompanied and supported that lifestyle. They plundered freely, without regard or responsibility to the Great Provider and care of the source, respectively.

The invaders' treatment of the land and its resources were shocking to the natives and disgusting even to some of their own. Historian William Strickland wrote a first-hand account of what he witnessed in his *Journal of a Tour of the United States of America 1794-1795*, and described the settlors as having:

"an utter abhorrence for the works of creation that exist on the place where he unfortunately settles himself. In the first place he drives away or destroys the more humanized Savage the rightful proprietor of the soil; in the next place he thoughtlessly and rapaciously exterminates all living animals, that can afford profit, or maintenance to man, he then extirpates the woods that cloath and ornament the country, and that to any but himself would be of the greatest value, and finally he exhausts and wears out the soil, and with the devasta-tion he has thus committed usually meets with his own ruin; for by this time he is reduced to his original poverty; and it is then left him only to sally forth and seek the frontiers, a new country which he may again devour....The day appears not too distant when America so lately an unbroken forest, will be worse supplied with timber than most of the old countries of Europe." (New York Historical Society (1971) Library of Congress No. 75-165767) [23]

This is a near-perfect description of the traits exhibited by many transnational CEOs today.

---

[23] *Quoted in The Great Work: Our Way Into the Future, by Thomas Berry Three Rivers Press, New York (1999)*

Our way forward as a nation will require not only that corporations return to the requirements and responsibilities of public service, but that all Americans accept the responsibility toward our homeland and Mother Earth that attends this freedom to live as we wish, which is a local concern.

The corporations that now own or control most of our natural resources, are drawing out that which took millions of years to concentrate in the earth, at rates that will utterly deplete them if allowed to continue. We are borrowing that which belongs to future generations, not us, and it is a debt that we cannot repay.

The same resources are on this planet that were here a billion years ago, but no more. We're drinking the same fresh water as the dinosaurs did over 200 million years ago. A rethinking of our approach to these resources is now necessary. It is incumbent upon us to develop new ways of dealing with the natural wealth of this land. The holding of all, or nearly all, of the natural resources of the land by that top .1% of the population, and 90% by corporations, cannot be justified by any logic or right.

Acceptable human freedoms do not extend to controlling the means by which others must live or the natural resources of a nation. The current model of over-extraction to the benefit of a very few, and to the detriment of the nation and future, is not a fair or sustainable model.

Economist Herman Daly (*Steady State Economics* (1977)) and other sustainable-living advocates have devised methods and market-mechanisms which our nation must seriously consider to correct the imbalances, once corporate control of our representatives in Washington, DC is broken.

That which man produces by his own labor is his without question, but the natural resources which must sustain us all can hardly be claimed by one small group and should never have been allowed under corporate ownership or control from the beginning. The market model that could be our nation's salvation was developed by Daly forty years ago and subjected to ridicule by other econo-mists, but many scoff no more.

Daly proposed that ores, oil and all non-renewable resources which must last mankind forever, should be priced *and* sold accord-ingly, and must include all costs, such as entropy, rarity, cost to the environment (both of extraction and waste on the other end). This true-costing model was to be based on the long-term needs of mankind rather than the next quarterly profit statement of a cor-poration. These commodities should then be subject to a bidding process over and above all true costs, and based on the long view of our world's needs, with the overage kept as close to the source as possible, under local control.

The extractor, processor, and the owner of the property would all be properly and profitably compensated for their part in the commodities' site ownership, removal and preparation. Limits based on estimated remaining resources should be considered to determine annual rates of extraction in protection of future gen-erations and their rights to those resources.

The resulting price of the commodities would then have a bid base which included *all real costs*, not just the temporal ones.

Profits realized from the auctioning of these commodities con-tracts would accrue to the benefit of the locality or state, to whom they belong, *and controlled at the local or state level.*

To protect those funds from being pillaged by politicians, their specific uses must be explicit and inviolable. If politicians have the power to borrow, re-direct, or spend them, it will be all for naught and end up like Social Security, which has been plundered. Not a penny remains.

The prices of these commodities, which include all costs, will spark the birth of a real effort to reclaim waste and recycle. The cost of recycling plastic or recombining its carbon and hydrogen atoms to use as fuel, will be more cost-effective than drilling and processing the oil from which it comes. The billions of tons of scrap metal will be more cost effective to reclaim than mining the remaining stores, which belong to future generations. The entropy factor of our existence will be reduced to a survivable level.

As water (mankind's most precious commodity) becomes ever more scarce or fouled, this true-value costing may be expanded to it as well, as suggested by the 1990s work of Tony Allan of King's College London, and more recently, by Dutch scientist, Arjen Hoekstra's work with UNESCO and the University of Twente.

For example, 1,857 gallons of water are required to produce one pound of beef (versus 469 gallons per pound of chicken). If the true cost of that water was added into the cost of a steak (or the 634 gallons required for just one hamburger), buying patterns and the demand for such environmentally harmful products would plummet.

If the actual footprint of such products was included, like the 18,700 pounds of feed it takes to produce that one beef steer, and the 20.9 square meters per kilogram it takes to feed and pasture it (approximately 61,354 ft2 for a 600 pound steer), the true cost would be prohibitive under current factory methods of production. Under a true-cost method, however, those who can't live without such products would bear the outrageous expense associated with producing them, rather than all of society.

The Cargill/ADM grain monopolies export billions of gallons of water belonging to *We the People* each year in their agricultural products, and at no extra cost to themselves or their profits. Paying the true costs, including our nation's water they are exporting, might allow third-world nations to become self-sufficient once again by growing their own locally-produced crops rather than being force-fed ADM and Cargill's government-subsidized products from the United States. These exports are drawing the underwater aquifers of the many parts of the United States which took thousands of years to fill, to dangerously low levels.[24] *We the People*

---

24 *May 20, 2013 (Reuters) – "Water levels in U.S. aquifers, the vast underground storage areas tapped for agriculture, energy and human consumption, between 2000 and*

lose on every pound of grain they export, while ADM & Cargill control much of the world's food supply.

The grain monopolies' displacement of local farms and farmers through underpriced products due to direct government subsidies and less direct advantages, such as using increasingly scarce water belonging to *We the People*, harms everyone. The big factory corporate farm is the most destructive to the environment and the most inefficient in terms of food production, per acre. In an article by George Monbiot, "The Small Farmer is the planet's best hope," in the Guardian Weekly (June 13, 2008), the facts make the point pellucid:

> "*Although the rich world's governments won't hear it, the issue of whether or not the world will be fed is partly a function of ownership. This reflects an unexpected discovery, first made in 1962 by the Nobel economist Amartya Sen and since confirmed by dozens of studies. There is an inverse relationship between the size of farms and the amount of crops they produce per hectare. The smaller they are, the greater the yield. In some cases the difference is enormous. A recent study in Turkey, for example, found that farms of less than one hectare are 20 times as productive as farms of more than 10 hectares. Sen's observation has been tested in India, Pakistan, Nepal, Malaysia, Thailand, Java, the Philippines, Brazil, Columbia, and Paraguay. It appears to hold almost everywhere.*"

By being forced to pay the true cost of production, and eliminating the direct and indirect subsidies the food monopolies receive from our federal government, they could not compete with the family farms they displaced and put out of business over the past century. A resurgence of small, diverse, and more productive farming could occur, greatly increasing the nation (and world's) food security while encouraging local production once more.

2008 dropped at a rate that was almost three times as great as any time during the 20th century, U.S. officials said on Monday."

This model of true cost calculation and payment to the real owners of the natural resources would also have a much needed dampening effect on the junk and consumer culture which feeds this drawing down on limited resources and unlimited growth of landfills. This sensible method could be applied to all corporate and industrially made products.

A pair of jeans, for example, requires 2,900 gallons of water to produce. One cotton T-shirt, takes 766 gallons. By pricing products to include these real costs and making that a paid cost to the nation by the *commercial* producers, the costs of gross consumerism would be paid by those who *spend, spend, spend* and *grow, grow, grow,* rather than by everyone, and should reduce demand significantly.

Waste, the manufacturing of unneeded junk, and the production of environmentally destructive products, would be reduced overnight by true cost allocation. A pool of serious money could accumulate to help those less advantaged of our citizens and to secure future resources of the nation for posterity. This is the sustainable way forward.

Junkyards would become the ore mines of the future and landfills the source of industrial raw materials, solving two problems at one time. New waste accumulation would be minimal and past waste would become profitable to recycle and reuse.

Technology *cannot* cure the fact that our planet's resources are finite. Technology *can* make their usage more efficient and effective, however.

Technology can harness unlimited power from sun, wind, tides to provide additional energy. New clean-coal technology (*Coal Star*™) provides for on-demand energy production, (and we have more coal energy under just the State of Illinois, than the entire Middle East has oil energy). Corporations will not deem these means to be cost-effective alternatives until and unless they are required to pay the true cost of the nation's natural resources that they are using up, burning, and squandering instead.

The nation's resources belong to **We the People** and our descendants, not to a handful of corporate giants who have proven to be scoundrels as their stewards. The *grow, grow, grow,* and *waste, waste, waste* model promoted by the corporatocracy and its two political parties in Washington benefits big government and big corporations only, and it is killing our homeland and future.

Technology alone cannot solve our problems. It is time for technological man and natural man to unite and forge a new model, which will require breaking the strangle-hold of government and its corporate rulers over **We the People**. At present, individuals cannot even create their own energy without difficult-to-obtain government or power monopoly permission. Catching runoff and rainwater is a crime in Colorado and other States, to protect those public and private entities that sell it. Such is wrong.

These silly laws and rules are not for the benefit of the public, but in service to those whom the lawmakers serve in industry. Without government and corporate interference, even devastated inner city areas such as Detroit and Cleveland could begin transformation to green power and urban food production. Freedom from restraint and a combination of technology with natural life are the answers. The most innovative reformations in these areas are those being brought about by individuals and neighborhoods in spite of their governments and corporate interests, which often throttle them.

Were these corporations unable to bribe our politicians, be they city councilmen, Congressmen, Senators, or the President of the United States, our nation would immediately transform to one run for the People and by the People, which brings us full circle. Saving our nation, quite literally, begins by taking back control of those who represent us, as laid out in Step One. Only then will Congress begin to look for actual solutions to our nation's problems rather than simply comporting to the whims of the corporatocracy to the detriment of the people and destruction of our environment.

The need for restraining big government and big corporate interests from decimating the remaining natural world and its resources has never been greater. The need for more local decision-making by those who must suffer the environmental damage on the one end of the cycle, and the waste and entropy on the other, has also never been greater.

Decisions must be made by those closest to their consequences, and by those who most suffer the effects of bad ones. Washington, DC is the last place for them to be made except for those that affect Washington. This will be part of the more sustainable way forward as well, and once the bribery of our national representatives in Congress stops, they will have less incentive to try to make such decisions. They will become more attuned to their constituents back home and their needs once the link of bondage to the corporations and professional monopolies is severed and bribery is again illegal.

The sustainable way forward is to make all citizens interested parties in the nation's future and protecting its national wealth in resources. Having a stake in their ownership would accomplish that.

ACTION PLAN

STEP 1- Establish natural resource commodities markets based on sustainable model, where all parties are paid for their parts in the process, but the overage, including the sustainability factors and auction profit, goes into a fund belonging to *We the People*, protected from pilferage by the politicians, for use to the benefit of the citizenry and future, rather than to select corporations.

CONCLUSION

The nation simply cannot survive on its current path. Effectively bankrupt since 1933 and piling up debt at trillions each year, while starting expensive offensive wars and running a costly police state, our nation cannot continue on this course without descending into total tyranny at some point. History stands as a ready reference as to the outcome one can expect. Governments such as ours has now become, usually evolve into being self-enfranchised. Their monopoly on force is used to sustain themselves at any cost, rather than for the benefit of those they were intended to serve. Collapse eventually comes to tyrannies over time, but it can take decades or centuries, which we and our environment can ill afford to grant at present. Change must come now.

The big government/big corporation model of gross consumerism which is instilled in every child in government schools and with every advertisement that assaults them during the day, is not survivable.

It is a physical fact that Mother Earth cannot continue to be squeezed, robbed, raped and pillaged of her *finite* resources for *infinite* growth. The stark reality is that current rates of plunder of her resources are far beyond sustainable levels already.

Mankind has bred and spread beyond the natural limits of our species. The irrational and unsustainable pattern of consumption promoted by the *corporatocracy* model, where dutiful citizen-consumers are told to go to the shopping mall to save the economy, will *grow, grow, grow* us into annihilation.

We are being driven upon the Malthusian horns by government and its corporate masters, in concert. [25]

---

25 *This is in reference to a treatise, "An Essay on the Principle of Population as it affects the Future Improvement of Society," written by English demographer, priest, and*

119

The waste and entropy factors of such a culture are also unsustainable. All of that unnecessary growth just to add a few dollars to the corporate bottom line, or to fund a new war on their behalf, becomes trash, sludge, wreckage, human waste, bodies, and poison on the other end.

Using the big government/corporate *grow, grow, grow,* model, we will drown in our own spawn and waste in less than a century.

These demonic Siamese twins of big government and big corporations must be separated and chained before they finish destroying the nation.

The first step toward beginning this separation process and decentralization of power is to devolve control back to the States, where it legitimately belongs, closer to **We the People**. No decision that affects how people choose to live amongst themselves is the province of federal government, constitutionally, so long as those local governments do not themselves violate the constitutional rights and privileges of the citizens in the process.

By taking back control of our representatives in Congress from outside entities and corporations as outlined in Step One, and returning the Senate to the control of the States and their legislatures as outlined in Step Two; this process can not only be accomplished, it can come about quickly. The return to our beloved Constitution will become a natural process of *devolution* after that.

And that is the beauty of our heritage. We don't need a *revolution*. We had the most beautiful design of government imaginable, and it happens to still be the law. We need a *devolution* to get back to our path and legal basis of federal government.

By restoring representation to **We the People** and the States (Steps One and Two, respectively), Step Three becomes more

---

economist, Thomas Robert Malthus (1766-1834). "While improvements in methods of food production tend to increase supply arithmetically, resulting increase in population tends to be geometric, leading to famine, war, and disease; or onerous regulation and 'vice' (as Malthus, a priest, termed abortion) to limit." These are the "Malthusian horns."

or less inevitable (A Return to Legal Sources of Revenue for Government). Federal government's hand can finally be extracted from our pockets and forced to reestablish constitutionally pre-scribed import duties and census-based payments from the States as its sources of revenue. This will have the two-fold effect of restoring jobs to America (and protecting them), while also limit-ing federal government's income so the beast may once more be restrained, *as designed.*

The next Step (Four: Returning to Constitutional Money) will stop artificial growth of the economy and restore stability. No more booms, busts and bubbles, where the bankers end up with almost everything in the end. Real money grows organically as real wealth is created. It cannot simply be printed like Federal Reserve notes out of thin air.

Removing the ability of government to rent this illegal, un-backed currency from the Federal Reserve, will stop the *false* growth bubbles, booms, and busts, thereby restraining the junk and consumer culture by limiting both the supply of money and its growth to that which is *real.*

The *grow, grow, grow* consumer culture requires fake money in order to exist. It cannot expand unnaturally without it. By elimi-nating the junk cash, we eliminate the junk culture. A true, sus-tainable, real-growth economy can emerge, where quality of life becomes the measure, rather than quantity of junk and trinkets. Real money also has the benefit of being impossible for govern-ment to steal through the tax of inflation.

Step Five, (Returning Government to Constitutional Duties and Limits), will occur organically and naturally once Congress is again beholden to its constituents rather than corporate masters and their cash, but this process can be driven forward now by tak-ing action at the State level.

Proposals such as Oklahoma House Joint Resolution 1089 (ref-erenced in Step 5), should be presented in all 50 State legislatures.

Federal government must be put on notice to cease and desist all activities not listed in Article I, Section 8 of the U.S. Constitution. Government is in breach of its contract with us and must be reminded that its employees are our agents, not our masters.

Such actions should be put in process now to drive the movement in Washington. Politicians will only get on board once they realize that the game is over, and *We the People* have had enough.

Step Six, (Returning the Executive to Constitutional Restraints), will be difficult until Congress has been retaken by *We the People*. The presidents have been allowed their illegal Executive Orders, unauthorized Justice Department, their 16 unconstitutional spy agencies, FBI, NSA and so on, because Congress has itself been so far out of constitutional bounds. Hardly any of its legislation or laws today are within the confines of the Constitution its members swore to uphold.

Until Congress has cleaned up its own act, it is unlikely to have any credibility calling the Executive Branch back into line. The presidents do not have the power to take the nation to war or to legislate with their unconstitutional executive orders and these illegal acts must end. Our first goal must be to get our representatives back to representing us, so they will do what is right rather than what the PACs, unions, corporations, and political parties pay them to do. Then, and only then, will we be able to force Congress to bring the Executive Branch under control, back within its constitutional limits, by impeachment and removal, if necessary. He (or she) is to be a figurehead, not a ruler or the "most powerful man on Earth" as is often said of the person living in *We the People's* White House. Wrong country.

Step Seven, (Returning Judicial Branch to Constitutional Function), won't happen until we've had several funerals of Supreme Court Justices and a complete change of heart in Congress. The current Roberts court and its members are there for life, and none of them appear to have ever read the Constitution as James Madison wrote it. The most difficult step of all, but the best long-term cure for our nation, is to find ways to replace them. We need some sensible, non-lawyer, constitutional scholars as Supreme Court Justices, not this endless string of attorneys who prefer to depend on bad *stare decisis* (precedent) and their own pettifogging, rather than James Madison's plain, clear words in the U.S. Constitution.

It seems to take a lawyer to misinterpret the United States Constitution and nine of them in black robes to completely ignore it. A non-lawyer wrote the Constitution, so it certainly does not require a lawyer to interpret its plain and clear language. The Supreme Court needs to get back ahead of the game, even if they have to move back into the basement of the Capitol to do it. Bad legislation needs to be stopped before it becomes bad law. With a budget of $6.97 billion (in 2012) the Judicial Branch could spare a few people to review bills out of committee and opine on their constitutionality upfront before they come to a final vote, rather than wasting more resources years later to overturn them. If Congress passes them anyway, the Court can be prepared to rule them null and void before they do harm.

Step Eight, (Restoring Military to Constitutional Boundaries), is not a recommendation to eliminate readiness or strength, as detractors will inevitably claim, but to make it better and legal. We were never meant to have an offensive force, only a defensive one. The most prosperous, peaceful, cleanest, *and* safest nation on earth was our example. This model has worked for Switzerland for half a millennia, in the midst of the bloodiest continent of that time period, and it can certainly work for us, isolated and protected by two vast oceans, with the world's strongest navy.

The military of today, through no fault of the fine men and women who serve in it, does not serve its intended purpose. It is little more than an armed escort for transnational corporations. It is too costly, has made us a pariah nation with most of the world, and is unconstitutional. We would be far better defended, and have far less reason for defense, if the federal armies reverted to State-controlled militias (Swiss model) as prescribed by our Founders, to be called upon in time of declared war.

Step Nine, Putting the Corporate Genie Back in the Bottle, is the underlying context of the whole plan. Our representatives were stolen from us almost 140 years ago by the predecessors of today's robber barons. Our currency has been debauched and our nation swallowed whole. We've gone from a peaceful republic to a warring empire in their service. Our nation is bankrupt and in decline with government's heel on our necks in the name of security, as recent revelations by NSA contractor Edward Snowden has shown.

I choose not to be their serf any longer. I will not have my children and grandchildren enslaved by them or sent to fight for their raw materials and die in foreign lands. Let them send their own, or do it themselves. I want to live in a free and peaceful nation, as is my inalienable right to do, which means one of us is going to have to go. This is my country. It does not belong to the corporations, and our government's contract is with *We the People*, not *Them the Corporations*.

It is time to take a stand. I want my country back.

Step Ten, (The Sustainable Way Forward), will come naturally to a free people no longer controlled by forces outside of their own communities and regions. Each State must decide for itself how to live, as intended: fifty separate experiments in self-government. Several States are re-asserting their sovereignty by refusing to enforce federal government's bizarre marijuana laws. Regardless of one's opinion on marijuana, it's a positive step in the right direction. I am against its use, personally, but will fight for another's right to do so, if they choose. In the nation's early days, growing hemp was required by the federal government of any landowner whose property was over a certain size to make rope for the navy. Now it's the cause of 49.8% of arrests and federal government wastes $42 billion each year trying to stop its citizens from using and growing it. It's a natural weed, and the number one cash crop of 12 States. Ridiculous federal abuses like this will ultimately lead to change.

Incorporating all Americans into the ownership of the nation's resources will make everyone stewards of the land. The great wealth of this nation can be shared by all those in it, giving everyone a stake. By applying free market and economic principles to the model described, this great land will have the means of supporting many more generations of Americans, sustainably. With the other changes implemented, we may return to freedom, but this time, freedom with respect and responsibility for our nation's resources, with shared responsibility and rewards as its stewards.

While it may seem almost impossible at present that these dramatic changes could come about swiftly in the United States, I respectfully disagree.

Those who were alive and watched the Soviet Union crumble under far less debt in August of 1991; know first-hand that it can happen. The speed with which that world power collapsed was a shock to everyone, but this is the natural, historic end to overly-powerful, top-heavy, militaristic, federal governments. The fact that we are us rather than them makes no difference to history or the immutable laws of economics, if we do not change.

Perhaps a better lesson to America's feckless leaders than the Soviet Union as to how swiftly their grasp on the nation can slip away from them is the current wave of mostly bloodless revolutions sweeping out the brutal dictators our leaders installed or have supported in Egypt, Tunisia, Yemen, Bahrain and Algeria, with more to follow. These U.S. backed thugs and their puppet regimes are falling like dominoes across the world as power returns to the people who do most of the living, working and dying in those nations, which is only right.

The winds of change are upon the world and Americans are not that far from finding power within themselves to take back their rights, their courts, and their government, from the same usurpers in Washington who have supported tyrants in other lands.

What is unique about this nation and what may yet save it, is the fact that we have a working plan for government, which is perhaps the finest and purest ever devised. It is also still the law. Our leaders just stopped following it.

Our current malaise, financial instability, unemployment, corrupt system of justice, unfair courts, packed prisons, pointless wars, as well as loss of industry and jobs are all curable now, if government simply returns to its lawful contract with *We the People*. That is all that is required.

We don't have to create a new government. We don't have to set up commissions to study the problems. We don't have to waste a moment, which is good, because we do not have a moment to waste.

Our design of government was basically perfect. We don't have to reinvent it, we just have to go back to it. All that is required to bring us back from the brink of disaster is to return to that design, get back on the path, and force the federal government to live by our contract.

We the People made a deal with government, and that "deal" was the United States Constitution. Our leaders are in severe breach of it, not us.

Want our nation to stop hemorrhaging money? Restrict federal government to its duties listed in the contract (Article I, Section 8). End of problem.

Want peace? Return to a constitutional military, which would require our presidents to quit murdering elected foreign officials and pillaging other nations. Force them to leave everyone the hell alone, and you've got peace overnight.

Want jobs? Put back our main source of constitutional revenue, import duties, which were designed to protect our domestic industries and jobs. America will become a boom nation in terms of manufacturing and employment in a period of months. No nation has ever free-traded its way to prosperity in history, and only the free-traders themselves are the ultimate beneficiaries of such madness. Put back this constitutional source of revenue and our nation will quickly return to full employment.

Want to end money in politics and return to a truly representative republic? It's Simple. Just do it. It is so easy. If only living, breathing citizens residing within the candidates' jurisdiction or district can donate money or services to those politicians, as was once the law, we are there immediately. No corporate money to buy them, no PAC's to lure them; no unions to threaten them, not even the two political parties could control the national agenda. Only individuals registered to vote or living permanently in the candidate's district can contribute. We're back to having representatives who actually represent, in one day. End of problem.

Want to keep our country from being stolen from us again? It can be done in three easy steps and it does not require a revolution. First, end federal government's self-granted power to tax individuals, by repealing the Sixteenth Amendment (or having it voided, due to the irregularities admitted in its implementation in 1913). Second, turn off the Federal Reserve's fake money machine by repealing legal tender laws and the Glass-Owen (Federal Reserve) Act. Go back to real money and allow people to create their own means of exchange. Third, return to the constitutionally required method of choosing Senators, who will guard the powers of the people and States from federal government's future attempts to usurp them.

If the United States federal government is required to live within the confines of constitutional sources of revenue (import duties, imposts, and excise taxes, with any shortfall allocated to the States based on the census) and we're using real money, government can only cause so much trouble. With the Senators once again elected by the State legislatures, things will stay in order this time.

Corporations do have their place, but corporations are *not* constitutionally protected from taxation as individuals are under Article I, Section 9. Once the anomaly of their citizenship is removed either legislatively or judicially, a straight 35% federal tax should remain on those operating across state lines, and whatever the States in which they were incorporated or operate set as their corporate rate. Those who wish to enjoy the benefits of corporate status and its protections can pay for it.

By having this tax on corporations, small entrepreneurs, privately owned businesses, and proprietorships, can once again flourish and compete, just as domestic industries will once more be competitive with foreign producers when import duties are re-imposed on foreign-produced products. The playing field is leveled and *We the People* are the beneficiaries this time, rather than *Them the Corporations*. This 35% corporate tax might even be considered the big corporations' *public service* that justifies their existence.

As can easily be seen, the United States does not necessarily need a *revolution*. It needs a *devolution*. Devolution is not regressive in this case; it is simply going back to what worked.

The beauty of this in the case of the United States is that we would be returning to our roots and living by our own laws for a change. This would act to put the true owners of the nation, *We the People*, back in charge of our lives and return us to being its natural beneficiaries. That would be quite a revolution, and nothing could be more American.

Perhaps our greatest challenge is also the easiest, which is taking back our courts from the prosecutors, lawyers, and judges who now control them through craft and deceit. Juries comprised of *We the People* are the rightful custodians of the courts and we must reassert our control over them. We not only have the power to judge the facts in the cases brought before us, we have the power to rule against any unfair, unreasonable, or unconstitutional law being applied in them, by refusing to convict those charged under such law.

We can nullify those bad laws and there is nothing any judge or prosecutor can do about it. We have the authority to completely ignore any instruction from any judge on any point of law.[26]

---

26 *By voting "not guilty", the law is nullified in a case, and that decision by a juror or jury is unreviewable. Even if someone is guilty of a bad law, it is the juror's and jury's*

In a jury box, we are the law and as a juror, have more power than the President, Congress, any legislature, or the United States Supreme Court.

All we have to do is reassert that truly awesome power and our courts will change overnight.

To aid in this transformation, Appendices D and E have been included. Appendix D is a questionnaire for federal jurors, which should be employed in making their decisions. Appendix E applies to jurors in State court cases and is therefore slightly different. These are the relevant issues historically considered by American juries in their deliberations prior to the courts being taken over from *We the People* and these considerations are still the proper ones for a jury, by law, to determine.

People charged under bad law should not suffer it.

Combined, these simple changes can restore our country to being a peaceful, prosperous, egalitarian, and free society. That is what we were meant to be rather than the biggest, meanest bully on the planet where only a handful of elites rule and own the land. That is what we rebelled from once before, and it is clearly time to do so again.

Not a single shot has to be fired, however, or a single drop of blood shed this time. We just have to make the current batch of tyrants understand that their game is over, and they are going to have to live by our contract once again. Government is going to have to follow the law–the ultimate law–our Constitution, or Washington Square may soon look like Tahrir Square did in February of 2011. It *can* happen here if they don't wake up soon. It *must* happen here, if they resist our calls for lawful government.

Our ancestors wrote to the last tyrant from whom we separated on July 4, 1776, "That whenever any Form of Government becomes destructive of these ends [Life, Liberty and the pursuit of Happiness], it is the Right of the People to alter or to abolish

---

duty to rule against that law by refusing to convict the person charged under it. This is part of our system of checks and balances.

it, and to institute new Government, laying its foundation on such principles and organizing its powers in such form, as to them shall seem most likely to affect their Safety and Happiness."

Those words were written by Thomas Jefferson, and can be found in our Declaration of Independence. The ills and injustices put upon our forefathers by King George III, pale in comparison to the abuses heaped on the American public by our leaders today, and it is clearly time to let them know that we have reached a satiety. It is time to go back to who we are supposed to be. It is time for America to return to being the shining light of liberty on the hill for others to follow, rather than the world's largest penal colony, with more laws, police agencies, prisons, and prisoners, than any (other) tyrant in mankind's history. It is time for us to once again live quietly in peace as we were intended to do, rather than murdering, invading, and intimidating those living in other nations, while being spied upon in our own homes by our own government. Those are not powers under federal purview or authority and those who exercise them in our name need to go.

It is time for us to get back to our own form of government, which is a *republic*, where we elect representatives, but there are certain inalienable rights that no majority can vote away, and no government can take from us. It is time for the American Devolution. It is time for us to return to our beloved Constitution. It is late in the day, but it can still be done peacefully. Let us pull together and save our country now, while that peaceful way is still open to us.

VIVA LA DEVOLUTION!

Howell Woltz, July 14, 2013

Photography by David Rosen

Journalist, Charlie Reese, wrote this article for the Orlando Sentinel in the 1980s. It has since been updated, amended and republished several times. It is fitting for where we are today in America.

545 PEOPLE

Politicians are the only people in the world who create problems and then campaign against them.

Have you ever wondered, if both Democrats and Republicans are against deficits, why do we have deficits?

Have you ever wondered, if all politicians are against inflation and high taxes, why do we have inflation and high taxes?

You and I don't propose a federal budget. The President does.

You and I don't have the Constitutional authority to vote on appropriations. The House of Representatives does.

You and 1 don't write the tax code, Congress does.

You and I don't set fiscal policy. Congress does.

You and I don't control monetary policy, the Federal Reserve Bank does.

One hundred senators, 435 congressmen, one President, and nine Supreme Court justices equates to 545 human beings out of 300 million (plus) who are directly, legally, morally and individually responsible for the domestic problems that plague this country. I excluded the members of the Federal Reserve Board because that problem was created by the Congress. In 1913, Congress delegated its Constitutional duty to provide a sound currency to a federally chartered, but private, central bank.

I excluded all the special interests and lobbyists for a sound reason. They have no legal authority.

They have no ability to coerce a senator, a congressman, or a president to do one cotton-picking thing. I don't care if they offer a politician $1 million dollars in cash. The politician has the power to accept or reject it. No matter what the lobbyist promises, it is the legislator's responsibility to determine how he/she votes. Those 545 human beings spend much of their energy convincing you that what they did is not their fault. They cooperate in this common con, regardless of party. What separates a politician from a normal human being is an excessive amount of gall. No normal human being would have the gall of a House Speaker (Tip O'Neill), who stood up and criticized the President (Ronald Reagan) for creating deficits.

The President can only propose a budget. He cannot force the Congress to accept it. The Constitution, which is the supreme law of the land, gives sole responsibility to the House of Representatives for originating and approving appropriations and taxes. House members, not the President, can approve any budget they want. If the President vetoes it, they can pass it over his veto, if they agree to.

It seems inconceivable to me that a nation of 300 million people cannot replace 545 people who stand convicted—by present facts—of incompetence and irresponsibility.

I can't think of a single domestic problem that is not traceable directly to those 545 people.

When you fully grasp the plain truth that 545 people exercise the power of the federal government, then it must follow that what exists is what they want to exist.

If the tax code is unfair, it's because they want it unfair. If the budget is in the red, it's because they want it in the red.

If the Army and Marines are in Iraq, it's because they want them in Iraq.

If they do not receive Social Security, but are on an elite retirement plan not available to the people, it's because they want it that way.

There are no insoluble government problems. Do not let these 545 people shift the blame to bureaucrats, whom they hire and whose jobs they can abolish; to lobbyists, whose gifts and advice they can reject; to regulators, to whom they give the power to regulate and from whom they can take this power. Above all, do not let them con you into the belief that there exists disembodied, mystical forces like "the economy," "inflation," or "politics" that prevent them from doing what they take an oath to do.

Those 545 people and they alone, are responsible.

They and they alone, have the power. They and they alone, should be held accountable by the people who are their bosses, provided the voters have the gumption to manage their own employees.

APPENDIX A

THE UNITED STATES CONSTITUTION

We the People of the United States, in Order to form a more perfect Union, establish Justice, insure domestic Tranquility, provide for the common defence, promote the general Welfare, and secure the Blessings of Liberty to ourselves and our Posterity, do ordain and establish this Constitution for the United States of America.

Article I

Section 1. All legislative Powers herein granted shall be vested in a Congress of the United States, which shall consist of a Senate and House of Representatives.

Section 2. The House of Representatives shall be composed of Members chosen every second Year by the People of the several States, and the Electors in each State shall have the Qualifications requisite for Electors of the most numerous Branch of the State Legislature.

No Person shall be a Representative who shall not have attained to the age of twenty five Years, and been seven Years a Citizen of the United States, and who shall not, when elected, be an Inhabitant of that State in which he shall be chosen.

Representatives and direct Taxes shall be apportioned among the several States which may be included within this Union, according to their respective Numbers, which shall be determined by adding to the whole Number of free Persons, including those bound to Service for a Term of Years, and excluding Indians not taxed, three fifths of all other Persons. The actual Enumeration shall be made within three Years after the first Meeting of the Congress of the United States, and within every subsequent Term of ten Years, in such Manner as they shall by Law direct. The Number of Representatives shall not exceed one for every thirty Thousand, but each State shall have at Least one Representative; and until such enumeration shall be made, the State of New Hampshire shall be entitled to chuse three, Massachusetts eight, Rhode-Island and Providence Plantations one, Connecticut five, New-York six, New Jersey four, Pennsylvania eight, Delaware one, Maryland six, Virginia ten, North Carolina five, South Carolina five, and Georgia three.

When vacancies happen in the Representation from any State, the Executive Authority thereof shall issue Writs of Election to fill such Vacancies.

The House of Representatives shall chuse their Speaker and other Officers; and shall have the sole Power of Impeachment.

Section 3. The Senate of the United States shall be composed of two Senators from each State, chosen by the Legislature thereof, for six Years; and each Senator shall have one Vote.

Immediately after they shall be assembled in Consequence of the first Election, they shall be divided as equally as may be into three Classes. The Seats of the Senators of the first Class shall be vacated at the Expiration of the second Year, of the second Class at the Expiration of the fourth Year, and the third Class at the Expiration of the sixth Year, so that one third may be chosen every second Year; and if Vacancies happen by Resignation, or otherwise, during the Recess of the Legislature of any State, the Executive thereof may make temporary Appointments until the next Meeting of the Legislature, which shall then fill such Vacancies.

No Person shall be a Senator who shall not have attained to the Age of thirty Years, and been nine Years a Citizen of the United States and who shall not, when elected, be an Inhabitant of that State for which he shall be chosen.

The Vice President of the United States shall be President of the Senate, but shall have no Vote, unless they be equally divided.

The Senate shall chuse their other Officers, and also a President pro-tempore, in the Absence of the Vice President, or when he shall exercise the Office of President of the United States.

The Senate shall have the sole Power to try all Impeachments. When sitting for that Purpose, they shall be on Oath or Affirmation. When the President of the United States is tried, the Chief Justice shall preside: And no Person shall be convicted without the Concurrence of two thirds of the Members present.

Judgment in Cases of Impeachment shall not extend further than to removal from Office, and disqualification to hold and enjoy any Office of Honor, Trust or Profit under the United States: but the Party convicted shall nevertheless be liable and subject to Indictment, Trial, Judgment and Punishment, according to Law.

Section 4. The Times, Places and Manner of holding Elections for Senators and Representatives, shall be prescribed in each State by the Legislature thereof; but the Congress may at any time by Law make or alter such Regulations, except as to the Places of chusing Senators.

The Congress shall assemble at least once in every Year, and such Meeting shall be on the first Monday in December, unless they shall by Law appoint a different Day.

Section 5. Each House shall be the Judge of the Elections, Returns and Qualifications of its own Members, and a Majority of each shall constitute a Quorum to do Business; but a smaller Number may adjourn from day to day, and may be authorized to compel the Attendance of absent Members, in such Manner, and under such Penalties as each House may provide.

Each House may determine the Rules of its Proceedings, punish its Members for disorderly Behaviour, and, with the Concurrence of two thirds, expel a Member.

Each House shall keep a Journal of its Proceedings, and from time to time publish the same, excepting such Parts as may in their Judgment require Secrecy; and the Yeas and Nays of the Members of either House on any question shall, at the Desire of one fifth of those Present, be entered on the Journal.

Neither House, during the Session of Congress, shall, without the Consent of the other, adjourn for more than three days, nor to any other Place than that in which the two Houses shall be sitting.

Section 6. The Senators and Representatives shall receive a Compensation for their Services, to be ascertained by Law, and paid out of the Treasury of the United States. They shall in all Cases, except Treason, Felony and Breach of the Peace, be privileged from Arrest during their Attendance at the Session of their respective Houses, and in going to and returning from the same; and for any Speech or Debate in either House, they shall not be questioned in any other Place.

No Senator or Representative shall, during the Time for which he was elected, be appointed to any civil Office under the Authority of the United States, which shall have been created, or the Emoluments whereof shall have been encreased during such time: and no Person holding any Office under the United States, shall be a Member of either House during his Continuance in Office.

Section 7. All Bills for raising Revenue shall originate in the House of Representatives; but the Senate may propose or concur with Amendments as on other Bills. Every Bill which shall have passed the House of Representatives and the Senate, shall, before it become a Law, be presented to the President of the United States; if he approve he shall sign it, but if not he shall return it, with his Objections to that House in which it shall have originated, who shall enter the Objections at large on their Journal, and proceed to reconsider it. If after such Reconsideration two thirds of that House shall agree to pass the Bill, it shall be sent, together with the Objections, to the other House, by which it shall likewise be reconsidered, and if approved by two thirds of that House, it shall become a Law. But in all such Cases the Votes of both Houses shall be determined by Yeas and Nays, and the Names of the Persons voting for and against the Bill shall be entered on the Journal of each House respectively. If any Bill shall not be returned by the President within ten Days (Sundays excepted) after it shall have been presented to him, the Same shall be a Law, in like Manner as if he had signed it, unless the Congress by their Adjournment prevent its Return, in which Case it shall not be a Law.

Every Order, Resolution, or Vote to which the Concurrence of the Senate and House of Representatives may be necessary (except on a question of Adjournment) shall be presented to the President of the United States; and before the Same shall take Effect, shall be approved by him, or being disapproved by him, shall be repassed by two thirds of the Senate and House of Representatives, according to the Rules and Limitations prescribed in the Case of a Bill.

Section 8. The Congress shall have Power To lay and collect Taxes, Duties, Imposts and Excises, to pay the Debts and provide for the common Defence and general Welfare of the United States; but all Duties, Imposts and Excises shall be uniform throughout the United States; To borrow Money on the credit of the United States;

To regulate Commerce with foreign Nations, and among the several States, and with the Indian Tribes;

To establish an uniform Rule of Naturalization, and uniform Laws on the subject of Bankruptcies throughout the United States;

To coin Money, regulate the Value thereof, and of foreign Coin, and fix the Standard of Weights and Measures;

To provide for the Punishment of counterfeiting the Securities and current Coin of the United States;

To establish Post Offices and post Roads;

To promote the Progress of Science and useful Arts, by securing for limited Times to Authors and Inventors the exclusive Right to their respective Writings and Discoveries;

To constitute Tribunals inferior to the Supreme Court;

To define and punish Piracies and Felonies committed on the high Seas, and Offences against the Law of Nations;

To declare War, grant Letters of Marque and Reprisal, and make Rules concerning Captures on Land and Water;

To raise and support Armies, but no Appropriation of Money to that Use shall be for a longer Term than two Years;

To provide and maintain a Navy;

To make Rules for the Government and Regulation of the land and naval Forces;

To provide for calling forth the Militia to execute the Laws of the Union, suppress Insurrections and repel Invasions;

To provide for organizing, arming, and disciplining, the Militia, and for governing such Part of them as may be employed in the Service of the United States, reserving to the States respectively, the Appointment of the Officers, and the Authority of training the Militia according to the discipline prescribed by Congress;

To exercise exclusive Legislation in all Cases whatsoever, over such District (not exceeding ten Miles square) as may, by Cession of particular States, and the Acceptance of Congress, become the Seat of the Government of the United States, and to exercise like Authority over all Places purchased by the Consent of the Legislature of the State in which the Same shall be, for the Erection of Forts, Magazines, Arsenals, dock-Yards, and other needful Buildings;–And

To make all Laws which shall be necessary and proper for carrying into Execution the foregoing Powers, and all other Powers vested by this Constitution in the Government of the United States, or in any Department or Officer thereof.

Section 9. The Migration or Importation of such Persons as any of the States now existing shall think proper to admit, shall not be prohibited by the Congress prior to the Year one thousand eight hundred and eight, but a Tax or duty may be imposed on such Importation, not exceeding ten dollars for each Person.

The Privilege of the Writ of Habeas Corpus shall not be suspended, unless when in Cases of Rebellion or Invasion the public Safety may require it.

No Bill of Attainder or ex post facto Law shall be passed.

No Capitation, or other direct, Tax shall be laid, unless in Proportion to the Census or Enumeration herein before directed to be taken.

No Tax or Duty shall be laid on Articles exported from any State.

No Preference shall be given by any Regulation of Commerce or

Revenue to the Ports of one State over those of another: nor shall Vessels bound to, or from, one State, be obliged to enter, clear or pay Duties in another.

No Money shall be drawn from the Treasury, but in Consequence of Appropriations made by Law; and a regular Statement and Account of Receipts and Expenditures of all public Money shall be published from time to time.

No Title of Nobility shall be granted by the United States: And no Person holding any Office of Profit or Trust under them, shall, without the Consent of the Congress, accept of any present, Emolument, Office, or Title, of any kind whatever, from any King, Prince, or foreign State.

Section 10. No State shall enter into any Treaty, Alliance, or Confederation; grant Letters of Marque and Reprisal; coin Money; emit Bills of Credit; make any Thing but gold and silver Coin a Tender in Payment of Debts; pass any Bill of Attainder, ex post facto Law, or Law impairing the Obligation of Contracts, or grant any Title of Nobility.

No State shall, without the Consent of the Congress, lay any Imposts or Duties on Imports or Exports, except what may be absolutely necessary for executing it's inspection Laws: and the net Produce of all Duties and Imposts, laid by any State on Imports or Exports, shall be for the Use of the Treasury of the United States; and all such Laws shall be subject to the Revision and Control of the Congress.

No State shall, without the Consent of Congress, lay any Duty of Tonnage, keep Troops, or Ships of War in time of Peace, enter into any Agreement or Compact with another State, or with a foreign Power, or engage in War, unless actually invaded, or in such imminent Danger as will not admit of delay.

Article II

Section 1. The executive Power shall be vested in a President of the United States of America. He shall hold his Office during the Term of four Years, and together with the Vice President, chosen for the same Term, be elected, as follows:

Each State shall appoint, in such Manner as the Legislature thereof may direct, a Number of Electors, equal to the whole Number of

Senators and Representatives to which the State may be entitled in the Congress: but no Senator or Representative, or Person holding an Office of Trust or Profit under the United States, shall be appointed an Elector.

The Electors shall meet in their respective States, and vote by Ballot for two Persons, of whom one at least shall not be an Inhabitant of the same State with themselves. And they shall make a List of all the Persons voted for, and of the Number of Votes for each; which List they shall sign and certify, and transmit sealed to the Seat of the Government of the United States, directed to the President of the Senate. The President of the Senate shall, in the Presence of the Senate and House of Representatives, open all the Certificates, and the Votes shall then be counted. The Person having the greatest Number of Votes shall be the President, if such Number be a Majority of the whole Number of Electors appointed; and if there be more than one who have such Majority, and have an equal Number of Votes, then the House of Representatives shall immediately chuse by Ballot one of them for President; and if no Person have a Majority, then from the five highest on the List the said House shall in like Manner chuse the President. But in chusing the President, the Votes shall be taken by States, the Representation from each State having one Vote; A quorum for this Purpose shall consist of a Member or Members from two thirds of the States, and a Majority of all the States shall be necessary to a Choice. In every Case, after the Choice of the President, the Person having the greatest Number of Votes of the Electors shall be the Vice President. But if there should remain two or more who have equal Votes, the Senate shall chuse from them by Ballot the Vice President.

The Congress may determine the Time of chusing the Electors, and the Day on which they shall give their Votes; which Day shall be the same throughout the United States.

No Person except a natural born Citizen, or a Citizen of the United States, at the time of the Adoption of this Constitution, shall be eligible to the Office of President; neither shall any Person be eligible to that Office who shall not have attained to the Age of thirty five Years, and been fourteen Years a Resident within the United States.

In Case of the Removal of the President from Office, or of his Death, Resignation, or Inability to discharge the Powers and Duties of the said Office, the Same shall devolve on the Vice President, and the Congress may by Law provide for the Case of Removal, Death, Resignation or Inability, both of the President and Vice President, declaring what Officer shall then act as President, and such Officer shall act accordingly, until the Disability be removed, or a President shall be elected.

The President shall, at stated Times, receive for his Services, a Compensation, which shall neither be increased nor diminished during the Period for which he shall have been elected, and he shall not receive within that Period any other Emolument from the United States, or any of them.

Before he enter on the Execution of his Office, he shall take the following Oath or Affirmation:–"I do solemnly swear (or affirm) that I will faithfully execute the Office of President of the United States, and will to the best of my Ability, preserve, protect and defend the Constitution of the United States."

Section 2. The President shall be Commander in Chief of the Army and Navy of the United States, and of the Militia of the several States, when called into the actual Service of the United States; he may require the Opinion, in writing, of the principal Officer in each of the executive Departments, upon any Subject relating to the Duties of their respective Offices, and he shall have Power to grant Reprieves and Pardons for Offences against the United States, except in Cases of Impeachment.

He shall have Power, by and with the Advice and Consent of the Senate, to make Treaties, provided two thirds of the Senators present concur; and he shall nominate, and by and with the Advice and Consent of the Senate, shall appoint Ambassadors, other public Ministers and Consuls, Judges of the supreme Court, and all other Officers of the United States, whose Appointments are not herein otherwise provided for, and which shall be established by Law: but the Congress may by Law vest the Appointment of such inferior Officers, as they think proper, in the President alone, in the Courts of Law, or in the Heads of Departments.

The President shall have Power to fill up all Vacancies that may happen during the Recess of the Senate, by granting Commissions which shall expire at the End of their next Session.

Section 3. He shall from time to time give to the Congress Information of the State of the Union, and recommend to their Consideration such Measures as he shall judge necessary and expedient; he may, on extraordinary Occasions, convene both Houses, or either of them, and in Case of Disagreement between them, with Respect to the Time of Adjournment, he may adjourn them to such Time as he shall think proper; he shall receive Ambassadors and other public Ministers; he shall take Care that the Laws be faithfully executed, and shall Commission all the Officers of the United States.

Section 4. The President, Vice President and all civil Officers of the United States, shall be removed from Office on Impeachment for, and Conviction of, Treason, Bribery, or other high Crimes and Misdemeanors.

Article III

Section 1. The judicial Power of the United States, shall be vested in one supreme Court, and in such inferior Courts as the Congress may from time to time ordain and establish. The Judges, both of the supreme and inferior Courts, shall hold their Offices during good Behaviour, and shall, at stated Times, receive for their Services, a Compensation, which shall not be diminished during their Continuance in Office.

Section 2. The judicial Power shall extend to all Cases, in Law and Equity, arising under this Constitution, the Laws of the United States, and Treaties made, or which shall be made, under their Authority;–to all Cases affecting Ambassadors, other public Ministers and Consuls;–to all Cases of admiralty and maritime Jurisdiction;–to Controversies to which the United States shall be a Party;–to Controversies between two or more States;–between a State and Citizens of another State;–between Citizens of different States;–between Citizens of the same State claiming Lands under Grants of different States, and between a State, or the Citizens thereof, and foreign States, Citizens or Subjects.

In all Cases affecting Ambassadors, other public Ministers and Consuls, and those in which a State shall be Party, the Supreme Court shall have original Jurisdiction. In all the other Cases before mentioned, the Supreme Court shall have appellate Jurisdiction, both as to Law and Fact, with such Exceptions, and under such Regulations as the Congress shall make.

The Trial of all Crimes, except in Cases of Impeachment, shall be by Jury; and such Trial shall be held in the State where the said Crimes shall have been committed; but when not committed within any State, the Trial shall be at such Place or Places as the Congress may by Law have directed.

Section 3. Treason against the United States, shall consist only in levying War against them, or in adhering to their Enemies, giving them Aid and Comfort. No Person shall be convicted of Treason unless on the Testimony of two Witnesses to the same overt Act, or on Confession in open Court.

The Congress shall have Power to declare the Punishment of Treason, but no Attainder of Treason shall work Corruption of Blood, or Forfeiture except during the Life of the Person attainted.

Article IV

Section 1. Full Faith and Credit shall be given in each State to the public Acts, Records, and judicial Proceedings of every other State. And the Congress may by general Laws prescribe the Manner in which such Acts, Records, and Proceedings shall be proved, and the Effect thereof.

Section 2. The Citizens of each State shall be entitled to all Privileges and Immunities of Citizens in the several States.

A Person charged in any State with Treason, Felony, or other Crime, who shall flee from Justice, and be found in another State, shall on Demand of the executive Authority of the State from which he fled, be delivered up, to be removed to the State having Jurisdiction of the Crime.

No Person held to Service or Labour in one State, under the Laws thereof, escaping into another, shall, in Consequence of any Law or Regulation therein, be discharged from such Service or Labour, but shall be delivered up on Claim of the Party to whom such Service or Labour may be due.

Section 3. New States may be admitted by the Congress into this Union; but no new States shall be formed or erected within the

Jurisdiction of any other State; nor any State be formed by the Junction of two or more States, or Parts of States, without the Consent of the Legislatures of the States concerned as well as of the Congress.

The Congress shall have Power to dispose of and make all needful Rules and Regulations respecting the Territory or other Property belonging to the United States; and nothing in this Constitution shall be so construed as to Prejudice any Claims of the United States, or of any particular State.

Section 4. The United States shall guarantee to every State in this Union a Republican Form of Government, and shall protect each of them against Invasion; and on Application of the Legislature, or of the Executive (when the Legislature cannot be convened) against domestic Violence.

Article V

The Congress, whenever two thirds of both Houses shall deem it necessary, shall propose Amendments to this Constitution, or, on the Application of the Legislatures of two thirds of the several States, shall call a Convention for proposing Amendments, which, in either Case, shall be valid to all Intents and Purposes, as Part of this Constitution, when ratified by the Legislatures of three fourths of the several States, or by Conventions in three fourths thereof, as the one or the other Mode of Ratification may be proposed by the Congress; Provided that no Amendment which may be made prior to the Year One thousand eight hundred and eight shall in any Manner affect the first and fourth Clauses in the Ninth Section of the first Article; and that no State, without its Consent, shall be deprived of its equal Suffrage in the Senate.

Article VI

All Debts contracted and Engagements entered into, before the Adoption of this Constitution, shall be as valid against the United States under this Constitution, as under the Confederation.

This Constitution, and the Laws of the United States which shall be made in Pursuance thereof; and all Treaties made, or which shall be made, under the Authority of the United States, shall be the supreme Law of the Land; and the Judges in every State shall be bound thereby, any Thing in the Constitution or Laws of any State to the Contrary not with-standing.

The Senators and Representatives before mentioned, and the Members of the several State Legislatures, and all executive and judicial Officers, both of the United States and of the several States, shall be bound by Oath or Affirmation, to support this Constitution; but no religious Test shall ever be required as a Qualification to any Office or public Trust under the United States.

Article VII

The Ratification of the Conventions of nine States shall be sufficient for the Establishment of this Constitution between the States so ratifying the Same.

Done in Convention by the Unanimous Consent of the States present the Seventeenth Day of September in the Year of our Lord one thousand seven hundred and Eighty seven and of the Independence of the United States of America the Twelfth

In witness whereof We have hereunto subscribed our Names, George Washington–President and deputy from Virginia

New Hampshire: John Langdon, Nicholas Gilman
Massachusetts: Nathaniel Gorham, Rufus King
Connecticut: William Samuel Johnson, Roger Sherman
New York: Alexander Hamilton
New Jersey: William Livingston, David Brearly, William
Paterson, Jonathan Dayton
Pennsylvania: Benjamin Franklin, Thomas Mifflin, Robert
Morris, George Clymer, Thomas FitzSimons, Jared Ingersoll,
James Wilson, Gouverneur Morris
Delaware: George Read, Gunning Bedford, Jr., John Dickinson,
Richard Bassett, Jacob Broom
Maryland: James McHenry, Daniel of Saint Thomas Jenifer,
Daniel Carroll
Virginia: John Blair, James Madison, Jr.
North Carolina: William Blount, Richard Dobbs Spaight, Hugh
Williamson
South Carolina: John Rutledge, Charles Cotesworth Pinckney,
Charles Pinckney, Pierce Butler
Georgia: William Few, Abraham Baldwin

AMENDMENTS TO
THE U.S. CONSTITUTION

Amendment 1 - Freedom of Religion, Press, Expression. Congress shall make no law respecting an establishment of religion, or prohibiting the free exercise thereof; or abridging the freedom of speech, or of the press; or the right of the people peaceably to assemble, and to petition the Government for a redress of grievances.

Amendment 2 - Right to Bear Arms. A well-regulated Militia, being necessary to the security of a free State, the right of the people to keep and bear Arms, shall not be infringed.

Amendment 3 - Quartering of Soldiers. No Soldier shall, in time of peace be quartered in any house, without the consent of the Owner, nor in time of war, but in a manner to be prescribed by law.

Amendment 4 - Search and Seizure. The right of the people to be secure in their persons, houses, papers, and effects, against unreasonable searches and seizures, shall not be violated, and no Warrants shall issue, but upon probable cause, supported by Oath or affirmation, and particularly describing the place to be searched, and the persons or things to be seized.

Amendment 5 - Trial and Punishment, Compensation for Takings. No person shall be held to answer for a capital, or otherwise infamous crime, unless on a presentment or indictment of a Grand Jury, except in cases arising in the land or naval forces, or in the Militia, when in actual service in time of War or public danger; nor shall any person be subject for the same offense to be twice put in jeopardy of life or limb; nor shall be compelled in any criminal case to be a witness against himself, nor be deprived of life, liberty, or property, without due process of law; nor shall private property be taken for public use, without just compensation.

Amendment 6 - Right to Speedy Trial, Confrontation of Witnesses. In all criminal prosecutions, the accused shall enjoy the right to a speedy and public trial, by an impartial jury of the State and district where-in the crime shall have been committed, which district shall have been previously ascertained by law, and to be informed of the nature and cause of the accusation; to be confronted with the witnesses against him; to have compulsory process for obtaining witnesses in his favor, and to have the Assistance of Counsel for his defence.

Amendment 7 - Trial by Jury in Civil Cases. In Suits at common law, where the value in controversy shall exceed twenty dollars, the right of trial by jury shall be preserved, and no fact tried by a jury, shall be otherwise re-examined in any Court of the United States, than according to the rules of the common law.

Amendment 8 - Cruel and Unusual Punishment. Excessive bail shall not be required, nor excessive fines imposed, nor cruel and unusual punishments inflicted.

Amendment 9 - Construction of Constitution. The enumeration in the Constitution, of certain rights, shall not be construed to deny or disparage others retained by the people.

Amendment 10 - Powers of the States and People. The powers not delegated to the United States by the Constitution, nor prohibited by it to the States, are reserved to the States respectively, or to the people.

Amendment 11 - Judicial Limits. The Judicial power of the United States shall not be construed to extend to any suit in law or equity, commenced or prosecuted against one of the United States by Citizens of another State, or by Citizens or Subjects of any Foreign State.

Amendment 12 - Choosing the President, Vice-President. The Electors shall meet in their respective states, and vote by ballot for President and Vice-President, one of whom, at least, shall not be an inhabitant of the same state with themselves; they shall name in their ballots the person voted for as President, and in distinct ballots the person voted for as Vice-President, and they shall make distinct lists of all persons voted for as President, and of all persons voted for as Vice-President and of the number of votes for each, which lists they shall sign and certify, and transmit sealed to the seat of the government of the United States, directed to the President of the Senate;

The President of the Senate shall, in the presence of the Senate and House of Representatives, open all the certificates and the votes shall then be counted;

The person having the greatest Number of votes for President, shall be the President, if such number be a majority of the whole number of Electors appointed; and if no person have such majority, then from the persons having the highest numbers not exceeding three on the list of those voted for as President, the House of Representatives shall choose immediately, by ballot, the President. But in choosing the President, the votes shall be taken by states, the representation from each state having one vote; a quorum for this purpose shall consist of a member or members from two-thirds of the states, and a majority of all the states shall be necessary to a choice. And if the House of Representatives shall not choose a President whenever the right of choice shall devolve upon them, before the fourth day of March next following, then the

Vice-President shall act as President, as in the case of the death or other constitutional disability of the President.

The person having the greatest number of votes as Vice-President, shall be the Vice-President, if such number be a majority of the whole number of Electors appointed, and if no person have a majority, then from the two highest numbers on the list, the Senate shall choose the Vice-President a quorum for the purpose shall consist of two-thirds of the whole number of Senators, and a majority of the whole number shall be necessary to a choice. But no person constitutionally ineligible to the office of President shall be eligible to that of Vice-President of the United States.

Amendment 13 - Slavery Abolished.
1. Neither slavery nor involuntary servitude, except as a punishment for crime whereof the party shall have been duly convicted, shall exist with in the United States, or any place subject to their jurisdiction.

2. Congress shall have power to enforce this article by appropriate legislation.

Amendment 14 - Citizenship Rights.
1. All persons born or naturalized in the United States, and subject to the jurisdiction thereof, are citizens of the United States and of the State wherein they reside. No State shall make or enforce any law which shall abridge the privileges or immunities of citizens of the United States; nor shall any State deprive any person of life, liberty, or property, without due process of law; nor deny to any person within its jurisdiction the equal protection of the laws.

2. Representatives shall be apportioned among the several States according to their respective numbers, counting the whole number of persons in each State, excluding Indians not taxed. But when the right to vote at any election for the choice of electors for President and Vice-President of the United States, Representatives in Congress, the Executive and Judicial officers of a State, or the members of the Legislature thereof, is denied to any of the male inhabitants of such State, being twenty-one years of age, and citizens of the United States, or in any way abridged, except for participation in rebellion, or other crime, the basis of representation therein shall be reduced in the proportion which the number of such male citizens shall bear to the whole number of male citizens twenty-one years of age in such State.

3. No person shall be a Senator or Representative in Congress, or elector of President and Vice-President, or hold any office, civil or military, under the United States, or under any State, who, having previously taken an oath, as a member of Congress, or as an officer of the United States, or as a member of any State legislature, or as an executive or judicial officer of any State, to support the Constitution of the United States, shall have engaged in insurrection or rebellion against the same, or given aid or comfort to the enemies thereof. But Congress may by a vote of two-thirds of each House, remove such disability.

4. The validity of the public debt of the United States, authorized by law, including debts incurred for payment of pensions and bounties for services in suppressing insurrection or rebellion, shall not be questioned. But neither the United States nor any State shall assume or pay any debt or obligation incurred in aid of insurrection or rebellion against the United States, or any claim for the loss or emancipation of any slave; but all such debts, obligations and claims shall be held illegal and void.

5. The Congress shall have power to enforce, by appropriate legislation, the provisions of this article.

Amendment 15 - Race No Bar to Vote.
1. The right of citizens of the United States to vote shall not be denied or abridged by the United States or by any State on account of race, color, or previous condition of servitude.

2. The Congress shall have power to enforce this article by appropriate legislation.

Amendment 16 - Status of Income Tax Clarified. The Congress shall have power to lay and collect taxes on incomes, from whatever source derived, without apportionment among the several States, and without regard to any census or enumeration.

Amendment 17 - Senators Elected by Popular Vote. The Senate of the United States shall be composed of two Senators from each State, elected by the people thereof, for six years; and each Senator shall have one vote. The electors in each State shall have the qualifications requisite for electors of the most numerous branch of the State legislatures.

When vacancies happen in the representation of any State in the Senate, the executive authority of such State shall issue writs of election to fill such vacancies: Provided, That the legislature of any State may empower the executive thereof to make temporary appointments until the people fill the vacancies by election as the legislature may direct.

This amendment shall not be so construed as to affect the election or term of any Senator chosen before it becomes valid as part of the Constitution.

Amendment 18 - Liquor Abolished.
1. After one year from the ratification of this article the manufacture, sale, or transportation of intoxicating liquors within, the importation thereof into, or the exportation thereof from the United States and all territory subject to the jurisdiction thereof for beverage purposes is hereby prohibited.

2. The Congress and the several States shall have concurrent power to enforce this article by appropriate legislation.

3. This article shall be inoperative unless it shall have been ratified as an amendment to the Constitution by the legislatures of the several States, as provided in the Constitution, within seven years from the date of the submission hereof to the States by the Congress.

Amendment 19 - Women's Suffrage. The right of citizens of the United States to vote shall not be denied or abridged by the United States or by any State on account of sex.

Congress shall have power to enforce this article by appropriate legislation.

Amendment 20 - Presidential, Congressional Terms.
1. The terms of the President and Vice President shall end at noon on the 20th day of January, and the terms of Senators and Representatives at noon on the 3d day of January, of the years in which such terms would have ended if this article had not been ratified; and the terms of their successors shall then begin.

2. The Congress shall assemble at least once in every year, and such meeting shall begin at noon on the 3d day of January, unless they shall by law appoint a different day.

3. If, at the time fixed for the beginning of the term of the President, the President elect shall have died, the Vice President elect shall become President. If a President shall not have been chosen before the time fixed for the beginning of his term, or if the President elect shall have failed to qualify, then the Vice President elect shall act as President until a President shall have qualified; and the Congress may by law provide for the case wherein neither a President elect nor a Vice President elect shall have qualified, declaring who shall then act as President, or the manner in which one who is to act shall be selected, and such person shall act accordingly until a President or Vice President shall have qualified.

4. The Congress may by law provide for the case of the death of any of the persons from whom the House of Representatives may choose a President whenever the right of choice shall have devolved upon them, and for the case of the death of any of the persons from whom the Senate may choose a Vice President whenever the right of choice shall have devolved upon them.

5. Sections 1 and 2 shall take effect on the 15th day of October following the ratification of this article.

6. This article shall be inoperative unless it shall have been ratified as an amendment to the Constitution by the legislatures of three-fourths of the several States within seven years from the date of its submission.

Amendment 21 - Amendment 18 Repealed.
1. The eighteenth article of amendment to the Constitution of the United States is hereby repealed.

2. The transportation or importation into any State, Territory, or possession of the United States for delivery or use therein of intoxicating liquors, in violation of the laws thereof, is hereby prohibited.

3. The article shall be inoperative unless it shall have been ratified as an amendment to the Constitution by conventions in the several States, as provided in the Constitution, within seven years from the date of the submission hereof to the States by the Congress.

Amendment 22 - Presidential Term Limits.
1. No person shall be elected to the office of the President more than twice, and no person who has held the office of President, or acted as President, for more than two years of a term to which some other person was elected President shall be elected to the office of the President more than once. But this Article shall not apply to any person holding the office of President, when this Article was proposed by the Congress, and shall not prevent any person who may be holding the office of President, or acting as President, during the term within which this Article becomes operative from holding the office of President or acting as President during the remainder of such term.

2. This article shall be inoperative unless it shall have been ratified as an amendment to the Constitution by the legislatures of three-fourths of the several States within seven years from the date of its submission to the States by the Congress.

Amendment 23 - Presidential Vote for District of Columbia.
1. The District constituting the seat of Government of the United States shall appoint in such manner as the Congress may direct: A number of electors of President and Vice President equal to the whole number of Senators and Representatives in Congress to which the District would be entitled if it were a State, but in no event more than the least populous State; they shall be in addition to those appointed by the States, but they shall be considered, for the purposes of the election of President and Vice President, to be electors appointed by a State; and they shall meet in the District and perform such duties as provided by the twelfth article of amendment.

2. The Congress shall have power to enforce this article by appropriate legislation.

Amendment 24 - Poll Tax Barred.
1. The right of citizens of the United States to vote in any primary or other election for President or Vice President, for electors for President or Vice President, or for Senator or Representative in Congress, shall not be denied or abridged by the United States or any State by reason of failure to pay any poll tax or other tax.

2. The Congress shall have power to enforce this article by appropriate legislation.

Amendment 25 - Presidential Disability and Succession.
1. In case of the removal of the President from office or of his death or resignation, the Vice President shall become President.

2. Whenever there is a vacancy in the office of the Vice President, the President shall nominate a Vice President who shall take office upon confirmation by a majority vote of both Houses of Congress.

3. Whenever the President transmits to the President pro tempore of the Senate and the Speaker of the House of Representatives his written declaration that he is unable to discharge the powers and duties of his office, and until he transmits to them a written declaration to the contrary, such powers and duties shall be discharged by the Vice President as Acting President.

4. Whenever the Vice President and a majority of either the principal officers of the executive departments or of such other body as Congress may by law provide, transmit to the President pro tempore of the Senate and the Speaker of the House of Representatives their written declaration that the President is unable to discharge the powers and duties of his office, the Vice President shall immediately assume the powers and duties of the office as Acting President.

Thereafter, when the President transmits to the President pro tempore of the Senate and the Speaker of the House of Representatives his written declaration that no inability exists, he shall resume the powers and duties of his office unless the Vice President and a majority of either the principal officers of the executive department or of such other body as Congress may by law provide, transmit within four days to the President pro tempore of the Senate and the Speaker of the House of Representatives their written declaration that the President is unable to discharge the powers and duties of his office. Thereupon Congress shall decide the issue, assembling within forty eight hours for that purpose if not in session. If the Congress, within twenty one days after receipt of the latter written declaration, or, if Congress is not in session, within twenty one days after Congress is required to assemble, determines by two thirds vote of both Houses that the President is unable to discharge the powers and duties of his office, the Vice President shall continue to discharge the same as Acting President; otherwise, the President shall resume the powers and duties of his office.

Amendment 26 - Voting Age Set to 18 Years.
1. The right of citizens of the United States, who are eighteen years of age or older, to vote shall not be denied or abridged by the United States or by any State on account of age.

2. The Congress shall have power to enforce this article by appropriate legislation.

Amendment 27 - Limiting Changes to Congressional Pay. No law, varying the compensation for the services of the Senators and Representatives, shall take effect, until an election of Representatives shall have intervened.

AMENDMENT 14 AS APPLIED TO CORPORATIONS [EQUAL PROTECTION]

Section 1- "All persons born or naturalized in the United States, and subject to the jurisdiction thereof, are citizens of the United States where they reside. No State shall make or enforce any law which shall abridge the privileges or immunities citizens of the United States, nor shall any State deprive any person of life, liberty, property, without due process of law; nor deny to any person within its jurisdiction the equal protection of the laws."

b. Business Corporations

1602. Generally

Corporation is as much entitled to equal protection of laws as individual. Frost v Corporation Com. of Oklahoma (1929) 278 US 515, 73 L Ed 483, 49, S Ct 235; Louis K. Uggett Co. v Lee (1933) 288 US 5I7, 77 L Ed 929, 53 S Ct 481, 85 ALR 699.

1603. Corporation as person

Corporation is person within meaning of Fourteenth Amendment which forbids state to deny to any person within its jurisdiction equal protection of laws. Santa Clara County v Southern P. R. Co. (1886) 118 US 394, 30 L Ed 118, 6 S Ct 1132;

Pembina Consol. Silver Mining & Milling Co. v Pennsylvania (1888) 125 US 181, 31 L Ed 650, 8 S, Ct 737; Missouri P. R. Co. v Mackey (1888) 127 US 205. 32 L Ed 107, 8 S Q 1161; Minneapolis & S. L. R. Co. v Herrick (1888) 127 US 210, 32 L Ed 109, 8 S Q 1176; Minneapolis & S. L. R. Co. v Beckwith (1889) 129 US 26, 32 L Ed 585, 9 S d 207; Charlotte, C. & A. R. Co. v Gibbes (1892) 142 US 386, 35 L Ed 1051, 12 S Ct 255; Gulf, C. & S. F. R. Co. v Ellis (1897) 165 US 150, 41 L Ed 666, 17 S Ct 255; Southern R. Co. v Greene (1910) 216 US 400, 54 L Ed 536, 30 S Q 287.

Corporations are persons within meaning of Fourteenth Amendment of Constitution of United States, and can invoke benefits of provisions of Constitution and laws which guarantee to persons enjoyment of property, or afford to them means for its protection, or prohibit legislation injuriously affecting it Missouri P. R. Co. v Mackey (1888) 127 US 205, 32 L Ed 107, 8 S Ct 1161; Minneapolis & S. L, R. Co. v Henick (1888) 127 US 210, 32 L Ed 109, 8 S Ct 1176.

Corporation is person within meaning of both due process and equal protection clauses of Fourteenth Amendment to Federal Constitution. Covington & Lexington Turnpike Road Co. v Sanford (1896) 164 US 578, 41 L Ed 560, 17 S Cl 198; Kentucky Finance Corp. v Paramount Auto Exchange Corp. (1923) 262 US 544, 67 L Ed 1112, 43 S Ct 636; Grosjean v American Press Co. (1936) 297 US 233, 80 L Ed 660. 56 S Q 444, 1 Media L R 2685.

Corporations may not arbitrarily be selected in order to be subjected to burden to which individuals would as appropriately be subject. Mallinckrodt Chemical Works v Missouri (1913) 238 US 41, 59 LEd 1192, 35 SCI 671.

1604. Corporation as citizen

Corporation has same rights to protection of laws as natural citizen. Home Ins. Co. v Morse (1874) 87 US 445, 20 Wall 445, 22 L Ed 365 (superseded by statute on other grounds as stated in Sverdrup Corp. v WHC Constructors, Inc. (1993, CA4 SC) 989 F2d 148).

APPENDIX C
AMENDMENT 16
[INCOME TAX]

"The Congress shall have power to lay and collect taxes on incomes, from whatever source derived, without apportionment among the several States, and without regard to any census or enumeration."

HISTORY; ANCILLARY LAWS AND DIRECTIVES

Explanatory notes:

The Sixteenth Amendment to the Constitution of the United States was proposed to the legislatures of the several states by the Sixty-first Congress on July 12, 1909, and was declared, in a proclamation of the Secretary of State, dated February 25, 1913, to have been ratified by the legislatures of the following states: Alabama, August 10, 1909; Arizona, April 6, 1912; Arkansas, April 22, 1911; California, January 31, 1911; Colorado, February 15,1911; Delaware, February 3, 1913; Georgia, August 3,1910; Idaho, January 20,1911; Illinois, March 1,1910; Indiana, January 30,1911; Iowa, February 24, 1911; Kansas, February 18, 1911; Kentucky, February 8, 1910; Louisiana, June 28, 1912; Maine, March 31, 1911; Maryland, April 8, 1910; Michigan; February 23, 1911; Minnesota, June, It, 1912; Mississippi, March 7, 1910; Missouri, March 16, 1911; Montana, January 30, 1911; Nebraska, February 9, 1911; Nevada, January 31, 1911; New Mexico, February 3, 1913; New York, July 12, 1911; North Carolina, February 11, 1911; North Dakota, February 17, 1911; Ohio,

January 19, 1911; Oklahoma, March 10, 1910; Oregon, January 23, 1911; South Carolina, February 19, 1910; South Dakota, February 3, 1911; Tennessee, April-7, 1911; Texas, August 16, 1910; Washington, January 26, 1911; West Virginia, January 31, 1913; "Wisconsin, May 26, 1911; and Wyoming, February 3, 1913.

Ratification was completed on February 3, 1913. The amendment was subsequently ratified by New Jersey, February 5, 1913; Massachusetts, March 14, 1913; and New Hampshire, March 7, 1913.

The amendment was rejected, and not subsequently ratified, by Connecticut, Rhode Island, and Utah.

INTERPRETIVE NOTES AND DECISIONS

1. Generally
2. Validity of Amendment
3. Relation to other Constitutional provisions
4. General scope of Congressional authority
5. Effect of state laws
6. What is "income"
7. Sales proceeds
8. Dividends
9. Insurance
10. Gifts
11. Government payments to railroads
12. Other
13. Who is subject to tax
14. State agencies and employees
15. Citizens residing outside country

1. Generally

Sixteenth Amendment does not extend taxing power to new or excepted subjects, but merely removes all occasion for apportionment among states of taxes laid on income from whatever source. William E. Peck & Co. v Lowe (1918) 247 US 165, 62 L Ed 1049, 38 S. Ct 432, 1 USTC 16, 3 AFTR 2971; Bowers v Kerbailgh-Empire Co. (1926) 271 US 170, 70 L Ed 886, 46 S Ct 449, 1 USTC ¶ 174, 5 AFTR 6014; Sprouse v Commissioner (1941, CA9) 122 F2d 973,41-2 USTC ¶ 9703,28 AFTR I, 143 ALR 226, affd (1943) 318 US 604, 87 L Ed 1029, 63 S Ct 791, 43- 1 USTC ¶ 9363, 30 AFTR 1087, 144 ALR 1335.

2. Validity of Amendment

Sixteenth Amendment was constitutionally adopted. Brushaber v Union P. R, Co. (1916) 240 US 1, 60 L.Ed 493, 36 S Ct 236, 1 USTC 4, 3 AFTR 2926.

In prosecution under 26 USCS §§ 7201 and 7203 for "willfully" attempting to evade federal income taxes and "willfully" failing to file federal income tax returns, defendant's views about validity of tax statutes, and Sixteenth Amendment are irrelevant to issue of willfulness and need not be heard by jury. Cheek v United States (1991) 498 US 192,112 L Ed 2d 617, 111 S Ct 604, 91 CDOS 305, 91 Daily Journal DAR 371, 91-1 USTC¶ 50012, 67 AFTR 2d 344, on remand, remanded (1991, CA7 HI) 931 F2d 1206, 91-1 USTC ¶ 50232, 67 AFTR 2d 965.

Action to recover sura paid on declaration of estimated income tax, was without merit, far-fetched, and frivolous, where based on allegations that Sixteenth Amendment was illegal because it placed taxpayer in position of involuntary servitude and that subsequent federal tax legislation had given rise to mass of ambiguous, contradictory, inequitable, and unjust rules, regulations, and methods of procedure so as to jeopardize taxpayer's rights as citizen by compelling him to assume unreasonable obligations and burdens to make just accounting of his income and pay tax thereon. Forth v Brodrick (1954, CA10 Kan) 214 F2d 925, 54-2 USTC ¶ 9552, 46 AFTR 515.

Sixteenth Amendment is effective legal document, even though only four states ratified its language exactly as Congress approved it—other versions containing errors of diction, capitalization, punctuation, and spelling–since, inter alia, in 1913 the Secretary of State declared it adopted, and Supreme Court follows "enrolled bill rule" providing that if legislative document is authenticated in regular form by appropriate officials, that document is treated as adopted. United States v Thomas (1986, CAT 111) 788 F2d 1250, 86-1 USTC 1 9354, 57 AFTR 2d 1215, cert den (1986) 479 US 853, 93 L Ed 2d 121, 107 S Ct 187.

That Sixteenth Amendment had been in existence for 73 years and had been applied by the Supreme Court in countless cases, was very persuasive on question of its validity; taxpayer failed to make exceptionally strong showing of unconstitutional ratification where he contended, inter alia, that of 36 states tendering Sixteenth Amendment ratifying resolutions to State Department, 11 states had adopted versions with different wording, 22 states had altered its punctuation, and one state bad actually rejected, it United States v Foster (1986, CA7 HI) 789 F2d 457, 86-1 USTC ¶ 9327, 57, AFTR 2d 1150, cert den (1986) 479 US 883, 93 LEd 2d 249, 107 S Ct 273.

Sixteenth Amendment was properly ratified. United States v Ferguson (1986, CA7 Ind) 793 F2d 828,86-1 USTC ¶ 9475,58 AFTR 2d 5179, cert den (1986) 479 US 933, 93 L Ed 2d 358, 107 S Ct 406.

Advancing argument, totally unfounded, that Sixteenth Amendment was not ratified by requisite number of states, will result in imposition of sanctions against taxpayer. Cook v Spillman (1986, CA9 Cal) 806 F2d 948, 87-1 USTC ¶ 9121, 59 AFTR 2d 665.

Arguments that Sixteenth Amendment was never ratified by required number of states because of errors in ratification process and that Secretary of State committed fraud by certifying adoption of Amendment are frivolous, in that Secretary of State is bound by State's notification of ratification, and respect for coordinate branches of government prevents judicial review of Secretary of State's official certification of ratification. Pollard v Commissioner, 1RS (1987, CA11) 816 F2d 603,87-1 USTC ¶ 9314, 59 AFTR 2d 1074.

Validity of ratification of Sixteenth Amendment is now beyond review, and petitioner's contention that be is uniquely qualified, as author of historical analysis of amendment, to make "exceptionally strong showing" required for evidentiary hearing will be rejected. United States v Benson (1991, CA7 111) 941 F2d 598, 91-2 USTC ¶ 50437, 34 Fed Rules Evid Serv 579, 68 AFTR 2d 5469, reh, en banc, den (1992, CA7) 1992 US App LEXIS 425 and amd (1992, CA7 HI) 957 F2d 301.

Frivolous challenges to 16th Amendment and income tax legislation and regulations will result in imposition of full range of sanctions provided by Rule 38 of Federal Rules of Appellate Procedure. Sochia v Commissioner (1994, CA5 Tex) 23 F3d 941, 94-2 USTC ¶ 50338, 29 FR Serv 3d 742, 74...

APPENDIX D
FEDERAL JUROR'S CHECKLIST

(Please share a copy with your fellow jurors)

Answer questions 1-7 to determine whether the defendant should be found GUILTY or NOT GUILTY; (assuming evidence proves guilt):

1. Was there *mens rea* (intent) on the part of the defendant to commit a crime? In other words, did he or she intend to do wrong in your opinion?
( ) YES ( ) NO

2. Does the law under which the charge is brought make common sense to you? In other words, is it something that a normal person would know should be against the law?
( ) YES ( ) NO

3. Does the law make it clear what behavior is unlawful? In other words, does the statute make clear what conduct is being made illegal?
( ) YES ( ) NO

4. Can the constitutional authority under which the law is authorized as a power of federal government to enforce, be easily recognized? In other words, can you find it in the list below, without having to stretch the meaning of the words?

These are the only areas authorized as the purview of federal government. If one applies, mark it. If none of them fit the law being applied, leave them blank.

( ) To regulate commerce with foreign nations, and among the several states, and with Indian tribes.

( ) To establish a uniform rule of naturalization, and uniform laws on the subject of bankruptcies throughout the United States.

( ) To establish post offices and post roads.

( ) To promote the progress of science and useful arts, by securing for limited times to authors and inventors the exclusive right to their respective writings and discoveries (patents and copyrights).

( ) To define and punish piracies and felonies committed on the high seas and against the laws of nations.

( ) To declare war, grant letters of marque and reprisal, and make rules concerning captures on land and water.

( ) To make rules for the government and regulation of the land and naval forces.

( ) To provide for disciplining the militia and for governing such part of them as may be employed in the service of the United States (military).

( ) To exercise exclusive legislation over the District of Columbia.

( ) To make all laws which shall be necessary and proper for carrying into execution the foregoing powers and all other powers vested in the government of the United States, or in any department or office thereof.

NOTICE- Powers of the federal government are limited by the Tenth Amendment, which states, "The powers not delegated to the United States by the Constitution, nor prohibited by it to the States, are reserved to the States respectively, or to the people." In other words, a law not falling reasonably within one of these listed areas, should not be enforced by a juror.

Does the law clearly fall under one of the duties of federal of federal government listed above?
( ) YES ( ) NO

5. What is the maximum sentence government can apply to each charge made?
Charge 1 _____months
Charge 2 _____months
Charge 3 _____months
Charge 4 _____months
      Total _____months
Is this a reasonable sentence for the alleged crimes committed? In other words, is this a sentence that you would consider to be "fair" if you or a member of your family had committed this crime?
( ) YES ( ) NO

6. If the jury finds the defendant guilty, what "enhancements" does government or the probation department intend to recommend to be added to the sentence?

Enhancement	Reason	Additional months
One	_____	_____
Two	_____	_____
Three	_____	_____
Four	_____	_____
Total	_____	

Are these reasonable additions to the sentence above? In other words, would you think them fair if you or a member of your family had to serve them for the reasons stated?
( ) YES ( ) NO

7. Was the court willing to give the jury the penalties, sentences, and enhancements sought by government against the defendant when they were requested?

( ) YES ( ) NO

SUMMARY FOR DETERMINATION

	YES GUILTY)	NO (NOT GUILTY)
1. Intent	_____	_____
2. Fairness of law	_____	_____
3. Clarity of law	_____	_____
4. Authority of law	_____	_____
5. Reasonableness (sentence)	_____	_____
6. Reasonableness (enhance.)	_____	_____
7. Transparency of court	_____	_____

If all seven items are "YES", the defendant should be found GUILTY.

If even one of the seven items is "NO", the defendant should be found "NOT GUILTY" according to the United States Constitution.

As a juror, you have the unreviewable right and duty to refuse to apply a bad law, or to allow an unreasonable sentence to be imposed (regardless of the judge's instructions). You can find a defendant "NOT GUILTY", and your decision cannot be questioned, nor can you be required to give any reason for your verdict. (See addendum to Juror's Checklist, Appendix F)

APPENDIX E
STATE JUROR'S CHECKLIST

(Please share a copy with your fellow jurors)

Answer questions 1-6 to determine whether the defendant should be found GUILTY or NOT GUILTY; (assuming evidence proves it beyond reasonable doubt):

1. Was there *mens rea* (intent) on the part of the defendant to commit a crime? In other words, did he or she intend to do wrong in your opinion?
( ) YES ( ) NO

2. Does the law under which the charge is brought make common sense to you? In other words, is it something that a normal person would know should be against the law?
( ) YES ( ) NO

3. Does the law make it clear what behavior is unlawful? In other words, does the statute make clear what conduct is being made illegal?
( ) YES ( ) NO

4. Is this law in keeping with the values of your community or your sense of fairness?
( ) YES ( ) NO

5. What is the maximum penalty the state can impose for this crime, and if it did so, would you consider that fair, and a sentence that you would readily accept if you or a family member committed the same crime?
( ) YES ( ) NO

6. Was the state willing to tell you the maximum penalty it was seeking?
( ) YES ( ) NO

If all of the answers above are "YES" and the evidence proves that the defendant was guilty, a juror should consider voting to convict.

If any of the above questions were answered "NO", then it would be improper to convict the defendant of a crime, even if the evidence indicates guilt. As a juror, you have the unreviewable right and duty to refuse to apply a bad law, or to allow an unreasonable sentence to be imposed (regardless of the judge's instructions). The defendant can be found "NOT GUILTY", and your decision cannot be questioned, nor can you be required to give any reason for your verdict. (See addendum to Juror's Checklist for case law on this point).

APPENDIX F
ADDENDUM TO JUROR'S CHECKLIST

Legal quotes on the power of an American jury:

"The jury has a right to judge both the law as well as the fact in controversy." John Jay, 1st Chief Justice, U.S. Supreme Court, 1789

"The jury has the right to determine both the law and the facts." Samuel Chase, U.S. Supreme Court Justice, 1796, and signer of Declaration of Independence.

"The jury has an unreviewable and unreversible power to acquit in disregard of the instructions on the law given by the trial judge." United States v. Dougherty, 473 F.2d 1113, 1139 (1972)

"The Jury judges the Spirit, Motive and Intent of both the law and the Accused, whereas the prosecutor only represents the letter of the law." CITIZENS RULE BOOK, Bill of Rights, Jury Handbook

"The people are the masters of both Congress and courts, not to overthrow the Constitution, but to overthrow the men who pervert it!" President Abraham Lincoln

"It is improper for a prosecutor to suggest that a jury has a civic duty to convict." Thornburg v. Mullin, 422 F3d 1113 (10th Cir. 2005)

"It is not only [the juror's] right, but his duty...to find the verdict according to his own best understanding, judgment, and conscience, though in direct opposition to the direction of the court." John Adams, 1771, Founder and second President of the United States. *The Works of John Adams*, by C.F. Adams, p. 253-255 (1856)

"The jury has the power to bring a verdict in the teeth of both law and fact." Oliver Wendell Holmes, U.S. Supreme Court Justice, 1902

"The law itself is on trial quite as much as the cause which is to be decided." Harlan F. Stone, 12th Chief Justice of the U.S. Supreme Court, 1941

"All the cases agree that the jury have the power to decide the law as well as the fact; and if the law gives them the power, it gives them the right also. Power and right are convertible terms, when the law authorizes the doing of an act which shall be final, and for the doing of which the agent [juror] is not responsible...It is essential to the security of personal rights and public liberty, that the jury should have and exercise the power to judge both of the law and of the criminal intent." Alexander Hamilton, Founder, Vice-President of the United States, and trial attorney, in case 3 Johns. Cas 336 (1804).

What Judges Don't Tell Juries
Minneapolis Star and Tribune
November 30, 1984

At the time of the adoption of the Constitution, the jury's role as defense against political oppression was unquestioned in American jurisprudence. This notion survived until the 1850's when prosecutions under the Fugitive Slave Act were largely unsuccessful because juries refused to convict.

Then judges began to erode the institution of free juries, leading to the absurd compromise that is the current state of the law. While our courts uniformly state juries have the power to return a verdict of not guilty whatever the facts, they routinely tell the jurors the opposite.

Further, the courts will not allow the defendants or their counsel to inform the jurors of their true power. A lawyer who made Alexander Hamilton's argument [: that a jury had the power to acquit simply because it did not like the law] would face professional discipline and charges of contempt of court.

By what logic should the juries have the power to acquit a defendant but no right to know about that power? The court decisions that have suppressed the notion of jury nullification cannot resolve this paradox.

More than logic has suffered. As originally conceived, juries were to be a kind of safety valve, a way to soften the bureaucratic rigidity of the judicial system by introducing the common sense of the community. If they are to function effectively as the 'conscience of the community,' jurors must be told that they have they have the power and the right to say no to a prosecution in order to achieve a greater good. To cut jurors off from this information is to undermine one of our most important institutions.

Perhaps the community should educate itself. Then citizens called for jury duty could teach the judges a needed lesson in civics.

Essay on Trial by Jury, by Lysander Spooner

Government is established for the protection of the weak against the strong. This is the principal, if not the sole motive for the establishment of legitimate government. It is only the weaker party that lose their liberties, when a government becomes oppressive. The stronger party, in all governments are free by virtue of their superior strength. They never oppress themselves. Legislation is the work of this stronger party; and if, in addition to the sole power of legislation, they have the sole power of determining what legislation shall be enforced, they have all power in their hands, and the weaker party are the subjects of an absolute government. Unless the weaker party have a veto, they have no power whatever in the government and...no liberties... The trial by jury is the only institution that gives the weaker party any veto upon the power of the stronger. Consequently it is the only institution that gives them any effective voice in the government, or any guaranty against oppression.

ABOUT THE AUTHOR

Howell Woltz is also the author of *Justice Denied: The United States v. the People*. Mr. Woltz lives and writes at his farm in Advance, North Carolina, in addition to speaking to university groups and organizations about constitutional and judicial reform in America. He is currently President of Woltz Media Corporation.

Mr. Woltz graduated from the University of Virginia in 1975 with a degree in economics, attended the Executive MBA Program at Wake Forest University, and studied at Caledonia University in Glasgow, Scotland. He has lived much of his adult life abroad as a trust and estate practitioner (TEP), founding two international banks, a trust company, a corporate management firm and two insurance companies. Mr. Woltz has advised presidents and prime ministers, but his passion throughout has been The United States Constitution and how his home nation could return to it.

Speaking engagements can be arranged through Woltz Media Corporation, or by visiting www.woltzmedia.com.

The Way Back to America is the culmination of 30 years of study on what went wrong in America, and how it can be set right again by returning federal government to the strict limits of it contract with ***We the People***. That contract is The Constitution of the United States.

Contact Information
Howell Woltz
Woltz Media Corporation
P.O. Box 2216
Advance, NC 27006
wwww.woltzmedia.com